Long-Range
Planning:
The Executive
Viewpoint

Long-Range Planning: The Executive Viewpoint

E. KIRBY WARREN

Associate Professor of Management
Graduate School of Business
Columbia University

PRENTICE-HALL, INC., Englewood Cliffs, N.J.

PRENTICE-HALL INTERNATIONAL, INC., *London*
PRENTICE-HALL OF AUSTRALIA, PTY. LTD., *Sydney*
PRENTICE-HALL OF CANADA, LTD., *Toronto*
PRENTICE-HALL OF INDIA (PRIVATE) LTD., *New Delhi*
PRENTICE-HALL OF JAPAN, INC., *Tokyo*

To Ingrid

Preface

For the last ten years, one of the most popular topics in business publications, conferences, and management development seminars has been corporate long-range planning. In this time, thoughtful executives have become increasingly aware of the need for developing a more systematic and effective approach to planning as a means of dealing with the ever accelerating rate, magnitude, and complexity of change which affects the corporation.

At the start, most of the writing and discussions were centered around the *need* for devoting more time and energy to formalized forward planning. These exhortations, particularly the ones originating in the business community, had an almost missionary fervor to them. Yet, the writers and speakers seemed to be at least equally intent on justifying the activity to themselves as to their audience, as has been the case so often in the past when something new and complex appears on the managerial horizon.

For the most part, this initial phase has passed. Writers, speakers, and their audiences now seem to have convinced themselves of this need and have turned their attention to the question "How do we go about developing an effective approach to formalized long-range planning?" Articles, conferences, and seminars on the subject, while they invariably begin with a brief examination of why planning is vital, now move much more rapidly and in far greater detail into the "how-to-do-it" stage. A plethora of cookbooks on corporate planning has been published in the last two years, and for those unable to digest a full book, a host of more specific "recipes" appears monthly, if not weekly, in the business journals. The American Management Association reports that registration requests for their seminars on corporate planning techniques have reached an all time high. As a past president of the National College on Planning, a branch of The Institute of Management Sciences, I have watched monthly TIMS meetings and annual symposia on "How to Plan" reach unprecedented popularity.

In light of this large and still growing number of seminars, books, and articles, the reader should ask, "Why *another* book on long-range planning? What will this book offer that has not already been covered?" In answer to these questions, this book may be distinctive in (1) what it *doesn't* try to do and in (2) what it tries to get business leaders to do by pointing out and clarifying the nature of problems which only they can solve. The reason for this departure is based on a firm belief that, no matter how learned the writer or seminar leader, *attempts to deal in depth with the "how to" questions are still premature.* After carefully reviewing the current state of the art, I do not believe that, at present, enough has been done by those in the best position to do it—capable, top executives who can provide meaningful answers to the "how to" questions. Despite the verbal interest in formalizing long-range planning, the state of the art is in its infancy.

Beginning with this premise, I have sought to clarify why a subject of such generally accepted importance has seen so little real effective growth in meaningful practice. While the nebulous nature of the area and its focus on a complex and constantly changing future contribute to the difficulty, this is not the major reason for so little progress toward sound practice. Tougher problem areas have been faced and dealt with far more effectively in the past: why not this one? In studying past managerial accomplishments, one basic factor appears again and again. Little or no real progress was made until top corporate executives were personally willing to commit a significant part of their energy and to adapt their behavior to the inherent requirements of the particular managerial challenge they faced. While major contributions have been made from the academic and consulting communities, the key wedge used to break through a new and challenging area for management has come from within the corporation itself. In observing current attempts to deal with formalized long-range planning, this wedge appears, with a few noticeable exceptions, to be missing. Thus, the thrust of this book will be an attempt to support this contention and identify the reasons which underlie it. By examining the misconceptions and obstacles which have prevented the wedge of top management effort from forming, it is hoped that they can be removed.

Toward this end, the book will begin with an attempt to reflect the importance of better long-range planning not merely to individual corporations, but to our national economic position and, in fact, to our free enterprise system. Chapter 2 will deal with the questions of what formalized long-range planning is and what it isn't, and with the related question of what constitutes a realistic set of expectations for it. In Chapter 3, three major roadblocks which impede true commitment of executive talent to developing a better approach will be analyzed in depth and an effort made to identify what must be done either to remove or to work around these roadblocks.

In Chapter 4, attention is focused on how the absence of effective means of measuring and evaluating long-range planning may lead to a variety of undesirable responses at operating levels to long-range planning efforts. Having pointed out through an examination of these responses what to expect when effective measurement and control do not exist, Chapter 5 seeks to pinpoint the deficiencies of present control devices. Why they fail when applied to long-range planning is studied in detail in Chapter 5, paving the way for developing in Chapter 6 an effective approach to measurement and control of long-range planning.

The basis for this analysis of the present state of the art has three parts. First, for the past eight years, I have sought to review carefully the writing concerned with long-range planning and related areas, such as diversification planning, merger and acquisition analysis, etc. Second, during this same period, I have been an active participant in and/or officer of numerous professional associations and university groups which have studied corporate planning in both theory and practice. Finally, I have conducted a study of corporate planning philosophy and practice in fifteen large corporations. This research involved more than three hundred hours of interviews with corporate and divisional management and additional hours of analyzing policy manuals, procedures, and actual plans.

In each company, several members of corporate management and key officers, in at least two divisions, were interviewed. Wherever possible, an attempt was made to identify two or more companies from the same industry with at least one regarded as doing a good job in long-range planning and another as not. Similarly, within each company the reason for seeking to study at least two divisions was to try to get one division which was viewed by corporate management as doing an outstanding job on planning and one which was having difficulties in this area.

To identify "strong" and "weak" companies within an industry, I spent four months interviewing leading consultants and academicians working with industry and attending professional meetings on planning and related areas. This groundwork not only helped select the companies to be studied but also was most valuable in providing me with (1) a better understanding of the subject prior to interviews and (2) contacts within the survey companies who would give me the time and candor so necessary.

To get this candor, it was necessary to assure those interviewed that neither they nor their firms would be identified specifically in the *text* of the book. The companies studied were:

1. A. C. F. Industries
2. American Cyanamid
3. American Machine and Foundry
4. American Radiator and Std. Sanitary

5. Colgate-Palmolive
6. DuPont (E.I.) de Nemours
7. General Electric
8. General Foods
9. International Business Machines
10. International Telephone and Telegraph
11. Merck
12. New York Central Railroad
13. Stauffer Chemical
14. Sylvania Electric Company
15. Union Carbide

I owe a great deal to the more than one hundred managers in these companies for sharing their experiences, successes, and frustrations with me. Thanks also to William H. Newman and Charles E. Summer, Jr., of the Graduate School of Business at Columbia and to Andrall E. Pearson of McKinsey & Company, Inc. for their support and guidance. Since my initial survey was begun under a grant from the Ford Foundation, I must thank that great institution for its support as well, while not binding them to any of the positions taken in the material which follows. My deepest thanks also to Marilyn Matthews for her work in preparing the many drafts of the study which preceded this one. Finally thanks to Professor David C. D. Rogers, Graduate School of Business, Harvard University; Mr. Walter B. Schaeffir, Assistant Vice President, Management & Resources Planning, Western Union Information Systems & Services, and Professor George A. Steiner, Director, Division of Research, University of California for their helpful comments and review of the manuscript.

E. KIRBY WARREN

Contents

4. Response of Operating Executives to Long-Range Planning Efforts   48

Measurement and Control: The Missing Link · How the Absence of Effective Measurement Undermines Long-Range Planning · Testing the Importance of Long-Range Planning—Test 1: Who is chosen as planning director and how is he treated by top management? Test 2: How much direct backing does the president give longer-range proposals? Test 3: What is management's response to strong and weak planning efforts? Test 4: How much emphasis is given to long-range planning in determining bonuses, promotions, etc.? · Summary

5. Measurement and Control: Why Present Practices Fail   61

The Management-by-Results Approach—Conflicts between management by results and long-range planning · Seeking to Modify the Approach · The "Planning Review Approach"—Preparation of one- and five-year plans at lower levels; Divisional summary, consolidation, and review; Corporate financial review; Substantive review of prose plan; Final review with corporate management committee · Conclusions

6. Measurement and Control:
Developing a Better Approach   79

*The "Concurrence" Approach at EDC, Inc.—The
planning procedure; The preliminary review procedure; The power of "nonconcurrence"; The post-
facto review procedure · The EDC Approach:
Summary · Using the Concurrence Approach in
Other Companies*

Long-Range
Planning:
The Executive
Viewpoint

1

The Unavoidable Choice:
Who Takes
the Initiative?

DURING the early stages of United States industrial development, the subject of long-range planning would have generated
little interest in business circles. In fact, the notion of trying
to plan very far in advance in great detail was contrary to both
the temperament of the entrepreneurs who built American
industry and the needs of the time. In a nation of unequaled
resources and unparalleled opportunity, isolated from the economic and political turmoil of Europe, long-range planning
was relatively unimportant. Many resources could be and were
squandered, and opportunities ignored because of their abun-
dance. The truly scarce "resources" were tough, hard-driving
men of action who had the capacity to organize the untapped
wealth of America to meet its growing needs.

During this period, successful business planning was
equated with management's skill in rapidly and economically
adapting to change. The relatively slower rate, magnitude, and
complexity of change permitted managers to wait until it had
taken place. Quick, imaginative *reactions* were often successful
substitutes for planning. In those instances where change made

adaption within a going organization impossible, the alternative of dissolution followed by the shifting of resources to more profitable endeavors could be accomplished with little real loss to either the business or the economy. The young and promising nation, like the young and promising individual, if isolated or at least insulated from the competition of more mature strengths, can afford to waste its resources and is probably wise not to allocate its energy to detailed long-range planning. In fact, this may dull its enthusiasm and drive.

The United States today is rapidly approaching maturity. It is no longer isolated or insulated from international competetion. American business no longer reigns supreme, unchallenged in efficiency and know-how. Both domestically and abroad, American businessmen have found that the increased speed, magnitude, and complexity of economic, social, technological, and competitive change make adaptation a costly substitute for real planning. These changes combine to make the decision-making process much longer, while concurrently shortening the economic or profitable life of any single business decision. Most business leaders recognize that the only way to meet this challenge, to shorten the decision-making process and to reach faster, less disruptive answers to changing conditions is through longer-range planning. For this reason, most of the executives interviewed agreed that a more formalized approach to long-range planning promises many potential benefits for the internal operations of their firms. They see it as a means to provide steady growth, availability of men, materials, machinery, and money when needed. They view it as a basis for minimizing costly crises. Typically, such benefits are conceived as means of reducing the day-to-day headaches of the executive's job. This is, however, merely part of the reason for the increased importance of corporate long-range planning. Before turning, in Chapter 2, to a more detailed analysis of what comprises a realistic set of *internal* expectations for long-range planning, consider the impact of corporate planning in the broader context of our economic system.

One of the clearest impressions gained from early interviews is that while the executives involved accepted the value of better long-range planning, few were satisfied with their company's ability to translate this value into meaningful practice. Each seemed, however, to take solace in the fact that while his company was not doing a very good job in this area, neither was any of his competitors. Frankly, this was quite accurate in 1958, and, unfortunately, there are relatively few exceptions today.

One executive commented that he often felt like the captain of a ship who ran feverishly from window to window on the bridge wiping away the steam caused by a faulty boiler. While wiping away the steam would not prevent the boiler from bursting, neither he nor his competition could afford the time to stop the engines to make repairs. He reasoned that while a few "boilers" would burst, most companies would manage to struggle along no worse off than their competitors. The fear that plagued this executive was that one of his competitors would figure out a better way to handle both the "windows" *and* the boiler.

The problems suggested by this attitude toward long-range planning, while serious for individual businesses, pose a far greater threat at the national level. In a world where international competition is increasing at an unprecedented rate, no nation can expect to maintain its economic position unless long-range planning is regarded as a necessity. The question which must be faced is that if the leaders of American business do not do this planning, who will?

The "boiler" is not likely to burst in our economic system because it has a number of "custodians" besides business management. We have, however, a choice, if management does not abdicate from its responsibilities, as to which will exert the greater influence in tending it.

The "Custodial" Role of Government in Meeting Economic Problems

The degree of concern for our present economic position by representatives of the federal government is reflected in the following statement: "The challenge in the next decade, arising from the combination of international and national problems which we face, is as serious as any which has confronted the cause of freedom since the democracies of Greece and the Roman Republic fell to the tyrants." [1] This statement was made by Senator Joseph Clark at the Tenth Anniversary Convocation of the Fund for the Republic, in January 1963, in the course of presenting what he felt to be the changing role of government in the economy. Speaking to the same subject and seconding Senator Clark's appraisal of the present situation was Dr. Gunnar Myrdal, world-renowned economist.

What makes both of their presentations of particular interest is not their common fears for the future, but their agreement on the most effective means of dealing with the problems they saw; namely, a greater dependence on the federal government. Before reviewing their prescriptions further, consider their diagnosis.

The Diagnosis

While both agreed that in a thermo-nuclear age the military threat of international communism was of prime concern, they focused the bulk of their attention on economic and ideological, *not* military threats. They pointed with pride to the success of the European Common Market and Japan but also noted that such success only served to highlight what Dr. Myrdal described as "the rut of relative . . . [economic] . . . stagnation" in which America finds itself today. The much publicized gold problem is still with us, and our economic growth until quite recently had been at somewhat less than half that of nations such as Germany, France or Japan. In fact, on a per capita basis, it was only slightly better than that of India. While most recent figures have shown us in a better growth position, it is difficult to determine the combined effect of the Viet Nam buildup and the recently "settled" squabble between France and the other common market nations.

---

[1] Joseph S. Clark, "The Role of Government in the Economy," a paper prepared for the Tenth Anniversary Convocation of the Fund for the Republic, New York City, January 22, 1963, p. 10.

Add to these gold and growth problems the several aspects of our difficulties in dealing with unemployment, and the problem takes on another dimension. Prior to the build up in Viet-Nam, the unemployment rate in the United States had held stubbornly close to 6 per cent for several years. While the overall rate is now down considerably, many question whether a reduction in the conflict in Viet-Nam would not send the rate back up to 6 per cent. Similarly many questions where an "unplanned" economy can deal adequately with the regional and structural unemployment that persists even today.

The Prescription and Its Implications

When one adds to growth and unemployment problems the complex question of how to make the most effective use of automation at approximately the same time as the post-war baby boom is being felt in the labor market, it is not difficult to accept the diagnosis of men like Myrdal and Clark. The accuracy of the diagnosis, however, does not speak for the reliability of what their prescriptions imply. To varying degrees, they cite the inability of an unplanned economy in general, and business in particular, to cope with the complex series of interrelated problems which must be faced in seeking stable economic growth. Myrdal stated, "What is becoming an urgent necessity in America is, in the first hand, a much better coordination of already existing government controls; i.e., their integration into a more perfect, deliberate and rational long-range planning . . . [and second] . . . the government will have to increase its responsibilities for a larger part of consumption and, consequently, of employment and production." [2]

To make this kind of direct and indirect action by government possible, Senator Clark sees a need for increasing the

[2] Gunnar Myrdal, "The Role of Government in the Economy," a paper prepared for the Tenth Anniversary Convocation of the Fund for the Republic, New York City, January 22, 1963, p. 3.

power of the executive branch to allow for faster action to
meet rapidly changing needs. He observed, "Jefferson was
wrong, that government is *not* best which governs least . . .
inaction is what the Founding Fathers intended—inaction until
such time as an overwhelming consensus was prepared for
action of some sort, inevitably a compromise of some sort.
They were right in their day. But they are wrong in ours." [3]

That there is a need for government to play a larger role
in assuring economic growth and stability is certain. Some
changes in the structure of government, such as modifications
of the committee system in Congress to provide for faster and
sounder action, are equally certain and desirable. But how far
can we go in the interest of greater growth and stability before adverse effects are felt on our social and democratic institutions? How far can we go before *this form* of quest for
long-range economic growth and stability damages the very
system—the competitive business system—which has been our
economic underpinning for a century? If there are weaknesses
in this underpinning, of course something must be done. Some
of the prescriptions, however, sound like efforts to strap a
weakened leg in a strong steel brace. The limb is supported
but eventually atrophies and is useless. Bind business if nothing
else will work, but first try harder to find means to build this
weakened limb, before taking steps which may lead to its eventually wasting away. But the blame does not lie with "power
seeking politicians" or "wild-eyed technocrats." In large part,
the single most important factor in determining the degree of
need for further direct or indirect activity by government in
the economic area will be the response of business to these national and international challenges.

Economic Planning—The Businessman and the "Objective Technicians"

Much of the increased pressure for more direct action by the
federal government in meeting economic challenge stems from

---

[3] Clark, *op. cit.*, p. 3.

the success of "Participative Planning" in many nations of western Europe. Consider the following statement: "We are engaged in a revolution of the mind, a turning away from the imitation of the past, toward an exploration of the future . . . to civilize capitalism—to cure it of the wild instability, financial crises, or spells of stagnation and unemployment that checks its history." [4] This commentary was made by the Director of the General Commissariate of Planning of a European country not long ago. The country—Russia? Roumania? Poland? The speaker?—a modern Marxist, no doubt.

On the contrary, the country is France, and the speaker is Pierre Massé, a man who considers his doctrine the antithesis of socialism and the only sensible way to meet the economic challenge of the communist world. Masse is joined in this be-lief not only by the leaders of the other members of the EEC or Common Market, but to varying degrees by those of both Conservative and Labor governments of Great Britain, other non-member nations of western Europe, and recently Canada. To meet the challenge of Marxist communism, these men have accepted one of Marx' basic propositions. Namely, that stable economic growth and an equitable distribution of wealth are impossible in a completely "free economy" and that, therefore, central planning is inevitable. Unlike the pessimistic prophet of a hundred years ago, however, the planners of western Europe feel that this planning can be carried out jointly by businessmen.

The success of economic planning in western Europe stems from a willingness on the part of business leaders to sit down with government planners and set basic goals for national eco-nomic growth. Based on these national goals, individual goals are set for specific industries. If the planners agree that more steel capacity and less capacity in the chemical industry is needed, new capital investment in these industries will be controlled through government licensing or differential in-terest rates to encourage growth in steel and discourage growth in chemicals. With the supply of capital going to each industry

---

[4] Pierre Massé, as reported in *Business Week*, April 7, 1962, p. 81.

regulated, the individual companies presumably compete just as before for market share. One may see advantages in such a system, but consider the details that now have to be left to the "enlightened forecaster" and "objective technician" rather than the market place. Such voluntary planning and cooperation seems most reasonable to those involved during a period of general growth and prosperity. Whether it can prevent a serious recession and what happens to the system in the event of such a recession are questions still to be answered empirically. Furthermore, as government becomes a full partner in such planning what are its obligations to business in the event of incorrect forecasts or recessions? What is the long-run effect on the competitive drive of individual companies participating in such a system?

The Price of Efficiency

The most basic question, however, if these prescriptions are to be tried in the United States is whether such planning can be carried out in a manner that is consistent not only with our economic system but with our social and political system as well. Massé recognized the problems when he observed, "The traditional values of the West, whether we call them humanism, Christianity, freedom, or the worth of the individual, now have come to grips with the problem of efficiency. We may hardly doubt that efficiency will win the day." [5] Yet, to achieve this efficiency, how much of our basic faith in the intrinsic value of the individual would have to be submerged? How much of our socio-political system based on the constructive channeling of conflicting individual needs and values must be changed? In short, how much will interest in greater efficiency dilute our basic belief in a pluralistic system which has jealously resisted the temptation to turn over to a governing elite the major responsibility for dealing with economic, political, and ultimately, of course, social issues? The nations of Europe historically have shown a greater willingness to trust the solution

---

[5] *Ibid.*, p. 83.

of their economic, political, and social problems to such an elite, whether feudal lords, enlightened monarchs, intellectuals, or out-and-out military dictators. The people of the United States, most of whom came to these shores to escape the abuses of such abrogations of individual rights, developed a political system which, despite the wishes of some of our Founding Fathers, made government by even a wise and beneficent elite virtually impossible.

Centralization of Military and Economic Decision Making

While in this age of atoms, space exploration, and international competition in economics, we face problems which go beyond the wildest dreams of our Founding Fathers, speed and conviction in solving these problems is not all that is required of effective solution. The magnitude of the probability to err now demands that the temptation to act quickly and forcefully be checked enough to make sure that the ultimate decisions are wise. But, what is the source of wisdom? Is not the collective wisdom of our leaders greater than the masses? In dealing with the complex economic problems outlined earlier, should we not, as a nation, rely primarily on the wisdom of the enlightened "expert" who represents the "public interest"? I firmly believe that the answer is no.

In the area of military defense, we have tended to move in this direction. The current administration has accelerated a long-run program of centralizing decision making in the defense department, designing it, so we are told, to operate rationally based on facts, not emotions. There is little room for interservice competition and jealousy. Committee type compromise is out. Facts are gathered, weighed out to the fullest degree possible by Secretary McNamara and his chief advisors, and the *right* answers are developed. The determination of what is "right" is based primarily on the "objective" data presented by men who presumably have no axe to grind and who are motivated only by their skills in solving complex problems so as to assure to the fullest degree possible the realization of what is best for the national interest. Further, the presumption is that all who must act to carry out these solutions will recognize that they are reasonable and will act in implementing them with the same dispassionate rationality that created them. Among the critics of the present pentagon prodigies is General Thomas D. White, former Air Force Chief of Staff, who recently commented, "I am profoundly apprehensive of the pipe-smoking, trees-full-of-owls type of so called defense intellectuals who have been brought into this nation's capitol." [6] On the other hand, Columbia University's Professor Richard Hofstadter observed, "Once the intellectual was gently ridiculed because he was not needed; now he is fiercely resented because he is needed too much." [7]

Thus, while the approach to defense problems presently followed by the Pentagon is by no means accepted completely, its successful emergence can be traced to three major factors. The first is the extreme importance of making the *right* decision. Failure to be right in a thermo-nuclear age is the second greatest risk a nation can run. The greatest risk is getting the right answer too late. Thus, the need for *speed* and *decisiveness* is so clearly evident that a highly centralized system equipped to make major decisions rapidly is vital. The third factor, however, is almost more important than the first two; that is, the administration's fortune in finding a man with the skills and temperament of Robert S. McNamara.

In matters of national defense we have always been willing to sacrifice, to varying degrees, our distrust of centralized authority and decision making and to subordinate pluralistic interests in the name of national interest. The question which remains to be answered is how far are we prepared to go in this direction, in the economic and ideological war we are carrying out with both the Communist bloc and the free nations of the world. In his Yale speech in June 1962, President Kennedy indicated that we must go much further than we

---

[6] Thomas D. White, as reported in *Business Week,* July 13, 1963, p. 58.

[7] Richard Hofstadter, as reported in *Business Week,* July 13, 1963, p. 58.

have gone up to now. When considering our problems with regard to economic growth and unemployment, the President stated that "the example of western Europe shows that . . . [such problems] . . . are capable of solution. That government, and many of them are conservative governments, prepared to face technical problems without ideological preconceptions, can coordinate the elements of a national economy and bring about growth and prosperity." [8] The promise of growth and prosperity must be applauded, but I find the implications with regard to the means of achieving these goals quite disturbing. There are, in my opinion, few things more dangerous or menacing to our present democratic system than the spectre of enlightened technicians facing "technical problems without ideological preconceptions."

Economic Change and American Values

Our fear of such an approach lies at the very basis of our free enterprise system. While our religious heritage has held that the most noble and desirable traits of man are charity and cooperation, our economic system is based on two directly contradictory traits, selfishness or self-interest, and competition. As a people, we have recognized that while charity and cooperation among men are always to be sought and hoped for, they are not dependable bases for ordering a large, complex, impersonal, industrial society. In a world of scarcity, a world in which many fail to satisfy psychological as well as physical needs, large scale "cooperation" must depend upon the "wisdom" and power of some central authority. Furthermore, the success of such authority is dependent upon its ability to direct according to a set of meaningful, universally accepted goals and values. By way of contrast, we accept the fact that in a pluralistic system in which the basic rights of man as an individual are held uppermost, there are few commonly seen

---

[8] John F. Kennedy, "Issues of Yesteryear," Commencement address at Yale, as reported in The New York *Times*, June 12, 1962.

and sought after goals that are also operational; that is, goals that can be attained and measured in a tangible, personal sense.

As a result, we have developed and maintained an economic and political system in which a more perfect realization of broad, national, and cultural goals is attained as an outgrowth of "selfish" striving by individuals to realize personal goals. This takes place in a mechanism which finds the individual simultaneously competing and cooperating with others who are engaged in the same process. We have come to distrust the completely rational man who has no axe to grind and is only interested in "truth." The injection into this system of the neutral technician who would make changes based on solutions which are not affected by "ideological preconceptions" will prove to be a most delicate one.

American Capitalism: A Dynamic System

To effect this injection in a manner consistent with competitive free enterprise is going to require no small amount of creative effort, and some change in the system itself is inevitable. We, however, have had to make many changes in this system in the past. A completely free economy never existed and certainly could not have survived the ideological challenges of Karl Marx. Capitalism has been modified in innumerable ways. To meet the challenge that competition must ultimately lead to the exploitation of labor and to the creation of monopolies, government supported the growth of labor unions and created a series of anti-trust laws. To meet the Communist challenge that a free market system would have to go through cycles of devastating depression followed by soaring inflation, government has blunted this danger through monetary and fiscal policy. Men like Adolf Berle, however, maintain that such indirect action by government is in this day and age wholly inadequate. It not only fails to assure general economic growth and stability, he feels, but in addition, it does little to assure a "wiser" allocation of resources within the system. Berle states:

> There is one national American economic system and . . . it rises and falls as a unit. A stiff miscalculation by the automobile industry in Detroit can throw off balance as large as essential industry as steel, incidentally forcing hardships on distributors, dealers, and small suppliers literally in every village.
>
> To avoid such fluctuations, he concludes that more direct state-corporate planning is essential.

He goes further:

> The profit motive . . . while it can produce without apparent limit, cannot allocate resources to certain kinds of needs.
>
> . . . The allied subject of this evolution . . . [in state-corporate planning] . . . will relate to allocation of resources . . . to those human activities which are not, and perhaps never have been, carried on within a private profit system. Medical care, good teaching, creation of an adequate supply of public servants who are scientists, doctors, or engineers—not to mention reasonable provision of decent instead of meretricious drama and art—all fall within this field.[9]

Again, as before, the assumption behind Berle's proposals is that there are "right" ways to do things whether they be stabilizing economic growth or allocating cultural resources. To find the "right" way, one need only turn these problems over to the technicians. The technicians will determine not only what constitutes the best balance of investment in steel and autos but what constitutes "decent" rather than "meretricious" drama and art. Such a notion seems a direct contradiction of the most basic tenets of American pluralism.

A system such as ours, which depends on the achievement of universal goals through a constructive, competitive quest

---

[9] Adolf A. Berle, "The Corporation in a Democratic Society," *in* Melvin Anshen and George L. Bach, *Management and Corporations, 1985* (New York: McGraw-Hill Book Company, 1960), pp. 81-83.

to achieve individual goals requires a great deal of informed disagreement. To compete vigorously and effectively becomes extremely difficult if, in fact, individuals or corporations spend a great deal of time trying to "understand" each other's needs and work to developing harmonious solutions. If we move towards a system which finds business and government spending more time together as understanding bedfellows seeking to satisfy common needs, then what will be the nature of the bundling board designed to prevent the conception of an economic Frankenstein destined to destroy its creators?

Seeking an Alternative

Obviously, there are weaknesses in the ability of our present business system to solve the complex problems of economic growth and stability faced today. Ways must be found to bring government still further into the act, because many of the problems of economic growth and stability in a world of unprecedented technological growth and international competition cannot be solved by private business alone. The proposals of Massé and Myrdal, of Berle and to a degree Senator Clark, however, seem in so many ways inconsistent with, not only our economic, but our social and political heritage that some other alternative must be sought. Wise men, men of vision, have raised questions in every age which were much like those of Massé, Myrdal, Berle and Clark. We have found in the past, however, ways of answering those questions which have not threatened the tenets of our economic, social or political foundations. We must find ways of doing this once more.

If there is anything more disturbing than the prescriptions of these men, it is the reaction of many business leaders to them. Charges of "socialism" and requests merely to let business alone and trust all to "good old American know how," produce much heat but little light. Who takes the initiative, especially with respect to detailed corporate plans, and external regulations in the United States is still unresolved. Given our heritage, it is still largely up to the top management of corporations to show by their actions, by their ability or inability to continue to take the initiative for maintaining our industrial position in the light of more complex economic conditions. The private corporation cannot ward off undesirable aspects of government participation unless it has its own house in order. Without better corporate long-range planning, private industry is in a weak position in terms of knowing what should and can be resisted and what should and can be encouraged in Washington. If one tenth of the energy now being devoted to fighting "further encroachment on the private sector" was devoted instead to finding more tenable means of supplementing private with public planning and translating the acceptance of the need for corporate long-range planning into practice, we might be well on our way to developing a more universally acceptable brand of twentieth-century capitalism. The remaining chapters of this book are devoted to this end.

2

The Nature
of Corporate
Long-Range Planning

WHILE thoughtful executives for many years have carried out in some form both long as well as short-range planning, the time periods considered and the comprehensiveness of the effort varied greatly with the situation and the outlook of the executive. Although certain key aspects of a business may have been planned with a longer time perspective, comprehensive corporate planning seldom extended beyond one year. When it did, it was largely on an informal, *ad hoc* basis. It was only in the last decade that a general trend towards developing formal, comprehensive long-range plans became noticeable. While this trend was accompanied by wide verbal acceptance in industry, there has been, as noted earlier, far less meaningful acceptance in practice.

The first and most basic obstacle interfering with effective development of corporate long-range planning stems from confusion about the nature of this activity and what should and should not be expected of it. The purpose of this chapter is to seek to clarify both the nature of the activity and to develop a reasonable set of expectations for it. Subsequent chapters will then deal with an exploration of the techniques and attitudes necessary to realize these expectations.

What Is Long-Range Planning? Some Common Misconceptions

To understand both the nature of present misconceptions about long-range planning and to pave the way for the position taken in this book, it is necessary first to consider the position taken by some of today's practitioners. Where they exist, these misconceptions fall into three basic categories. They are:

1. Confusion between long-range planning and one of its major parts or elements;
2. Confusion between long-range planning and one of the key areas in which it is required;
3. Confusion between long-range planning and one of its common characteristics.

As an example of the first type of misconception, consider the following comment by a division director of market research in a large industrial firm. When asked for his definition of long-range planning, he replied, "As far as I can see, long-range planning is long-range forecasting. You cannot plan unless you can estimate what the future holds. When I hear people talk about doing better long-range planning, this means to me to do better long-range forecasting." When the controller of the same division was asked for his concept of long-range planning, his reply equated long-range planning with an extended budgeting operation. This view was reflected in the responses of many top executives, particularly those with finance or accounting backgrounds.[1]

In addition, there were those who sought to define long-range planning in terms of other single key elements. Several

---

[1] John M. Thompson, Controller, Canadian Westinghouse, wrote: "Our modern concept of the budget is synonymous with planning and, in effect, represents a program for future action." "The Operating Budget," *The Controller* (July, 1956), p. 310.

top staff officers saw long-range planning as being essentially a matter of setting broad goals and strategies. On the other hand, to many line executives long-range planning was the process of making future decisions. To be sure, long-range planning involves all but the last of these elements, but it must be viewed as an activity requiring attention to all. It cannot be equated with only one of its elements, or it will suffer. It is not, however, a process of making tomorrow's decisions today, but rather *a process directed toward making today's decisions with tomorrow in mind and a means of preparing for future decisions so that they may be made rapidly, economically, and with as little disruption to the business as possible.*

The second common type of misconception about long-range planning stems from the tendency by some to define it in terms of only one of the key areas requiring long-term thought. To a number of executives long-range planning was, from a practical viewpoint, synonymous with diversification, or product improvement, or long-term financial planning. Again, by narrowing the scope of this major corporate activity, other areas of the business which have as great, if less evident, long-term planning needs are neglected.

The third type of confusion about long-range planning centers around the words "long range." Few discussions on the subject will last very long before the question arises as to what is meant by long range.

"When we talk about long-range planning, aren't we really talking about planning for contingencies?" one staff officer asked.

Or consider these typical comments:

"Though we call it long-range planning, we really mean planning designed to *change* major aspects of the business."

"Isn't it the breadth and potential impact of what is being called long-range planning that distinguishes it from other forms of planning?"

In these cases, the definer has usually been frustrated in his efforts to draw the line between long- and short-range on the basis of time and so he seeks to differentiate these forms of planning on the basis of some other key characteristic.

While most long-range planning efforts involve a high degree of uncertainty, seek to change something, are broad, and can have a major impact on the firm, not all long-range plans possess all of these characteristics, and it is conceivable that they may not contain any. Moreover, not all plans having one or more of these characteristics are necessarily long range. Consider for example an integrated effort to reduce inventory to avoid a third-quarter cash shortage. A plan is devised which will (1) reduce production for the next two months by 30 per cent, (2) increase daily newspaper advertising for the next six weeks to stimulate consumer purchases, and (3) provide for the first time a bonus discount of 3 per cent to distributors making large purchases during the next three months. This is all being planned despite a rumor, which cannot be confirmed at present, that a major competitor is understocked and will not be able to meet his full orders in another month. If this rumor proves to be true, the present plan will be an unnecessarily expensive method of reducing inventory. Such a plan includes elements of uncertainty, change, breadth and is designed to avoid a most undesirable cash shortage. Yet, the goals, actions, and impact of the plan are all quite short-run in nature.

The dangers of viewing long-range planning in terms of one of its major elements, or one key area in which it is needed, or to define it in terms of a "common" characteristic are several. Any of these views cannot help but limit the scope of the actual planning as well as probably unwisely influence the choice and interrelationships of key planning personnel. All of these factors must be recognized and given proper weight so as to provide the scope and perspective which will serve as the foundation for sound long-range planning.

Toward a Working Definition of Long-Range Planning

In and of itself, lack of a clear notion of what long-range planning is and what it can accomplish constitutes a major obstacle. In addition, lack of clear understanding can add significantly to the problems of those carrying out major elements of planning in dealing with the key executives who contribute to the planning process but who are primarily decision-makers who use and carry out plans.

The difference between planning and decision making:

It is not at all uncommon in writings and in management discussions to find planning and decision making treated almost synonymously. The distinction, far from hair-splitting, is an important one. Decisions must be made throughout the planning process on a variety of issues. For example, decisions are required on such questions as:

1. What problems or opportunities from among many should be studied?
2. What data should be collected and analyzed?
3. What assumptions and varying levels of objectives should be used?
4. How many alternative, action-oriented programs should be developed and analyzed?
5. What data should be used to support the recommended alternative?
6. How much and what kinds of managerial and financial resources should be used to carry out decisions on the first five types of questions?

While all of these decisions have a cost, none, including the last, involves any permanent commitment of large amounts of corporate resources. As a result, it is useful to distinguish this type of decision making from the type required after a plan has been developed; that is, decisions to commit resources to implementing the plan. This distinction considers planning as primarily a thought process involving ideas, words, and paper models. In contrast, the decision making which follows the development of plans involves allocations of dollars, men, and material and commits the company in the real world. Since it is taken for granted that line executives are the ones who make and administer these "real-world" commitments, it may also be taken for granted that they have to be the ones who do the planning. The provocative analyst Peter Drucker states in his book, *The Practice of Management*, that "Planning and doing are separate parts of the same job; they are not separate jobs. There is no work that can be performed effectively unless it contains elements of both . . . advocating the divorce of the two is like demanding that swallowing foods and digesting it be carried on in separate bodies." [2]

George Terry in his *Principles of Management*, while not supporting the position, however, states that in his judgment, "The sizable majority [of businessmen] feel that planning should be performed by one person and operating by another. Members of this school believe that most effective planning evolves when the planner is free of current operating problems and can devote his entire thinking to the vital function of planning. When both planning and operating are combined in one person both will suffer." [3]

Support for either position can be found in the literature but, frankly, this argument seems more a matter of semantics than issues. No one person in a corporation, nor does one group of people, such as line or staff, *plan*. Planning is essentially *a process of preparing for the commitment of resources in the most economical fashion and, by preparing, of allowing this commitment to be made faster and less disruptively*. To do so involves a host of very different activities requiring the talents and authority of many different contributors. Thus, to argue whether planning is a line or staff activity is next to meaningless. Consideration of who should carry out which parts of the planning process, in what manner and in what relationships, goes, however, to the heart of the problem and will be considered in detail in ensuing chapters.

---

[2] Peter F. Drucker, *The Practice of Management* (New York: Harper & Row, Publishers, 1954), p. 284.

[3] George R. Terry, *Principles of Management* (Homewood, Ill.: Richard D. Irwin, Inc., 1956), p. 129. Note: In his 1964 edition Terry or the executives have changed their minds, as he states merely that "many hold the position that planning should be performed by one person and operating by another . . . ," 238-239, 4th edition.

At this point we hold that most of the activities directed toward planning (not decision making) are and will be carried out primarily by staff specialists. Forecasting, data collection and analysis, the development of alternative programs and their support are by and large activities which most line executives delegate to staff. The line executive, in turn, provides more of the assumption and objective setting and should play a key role in directing the activities he does not carry out personally.

For planning to succeed these two groups must work closely together. If they do not, then much time is wasted as staff seeks to know what line wants and then "sell" its work, while line struggles to understand what the staff work means before being willing to commit resources based on the work. The more time and friction this process involves the less useful the plan. Again, any form of planning is primarily a process designed to permit economically sound decisions on resource allocation to be made more rapidly and less disruptively.

The need for *longer-range* planning is nothing more than a recognition that the economic lives of most decisions, today, are becoming shorter and, at the same time, the complexity of making such decisions is becoming greater. Thus, *more* decisions will have to be made with *less* time to correct them and making them will require more time and the coordination of more skills. This being true, the planning or preparation for the decision must start sooner and be oriented toward dealing with a more rapidly changing and, as such, less predictable future. Any loss in time resulting from conflicts between the technicians who do the bulk of the planning and the line executives who contribute to and use such plans defeats the purpose.

How Long Is Long Range?

While on the subject of time, a few words should be said about how long "long range" is. There have been numerous attempts to develop a meaningful time period which constitutes "long-range." Pulp and paper companies claim to do long-range planning on a forty-year basis. Companies producing products subject to rapid style changes consider anything beyond a year or two as being so unpredictable as to be irrelevant. In spite of these wide variations in what seems to constitute a meaningful time period, most companies have settled on five years as their long-range planning period. The best, in fact, the most reasonable explanation for this choice comes from Michael Kami, former Director of Planning at IBM and now in a similar post with Xerox. "We chose five years," he said, "because four years are too short and six years are too long." What he meant was simply that no arbitrary time period has meaning for all aspects of a company's activities. Thus, when selecting some period to use for formal, company-wide planning, five years "seems" right. The pulp and paper companies may develop plans on timber over a forty-year period but would scarcely dream of trying to plan their long-run marketing strategy for consumer products over such a period. Similarly, companies affected by style changes may consider one year long range in product design but should consider potential changes in manufacturing technology and plan for it over a longer period.

If planning is essentially preparation for decision making on the commitment of resources, the length of the planning period must be determined by (1) the time it takes to prepare for the decision plus (2) the time it takes to implement it in the light of (3) the time when implementation must be completed. For example, if it takes one year to prepare plans necessary for the development of a new product and two years to bring the product through prototype, testing, and production, and if the product must be ready for addition to the product line in three years, planning must begin today. If changes in consumer taste and present products indicate no need for this product for four years, there is no need to begin planning for a year. Similarly, if it takes six months to hire and train a new salesman, there is no need for detailed planning in this area more than six months prior to the anticipated need.

Why five years have become accepted:

If this is true, then why do most companies which have recently set up a long-range planning program seek to develop formalized plans for all phases of their business on a five-year basis? To get at the answer, consider why companies have historically developed formal, comprehensive plans on an annual basis, dividing the period into quarters (not thirds). Originally, it is likely that this was done simply because our calendar and recurring seasons provided some rationale for doing so. Undoubtedly, the advent of tax and financial reporting requirements played an important role in reinforcing this convention. What the executive realized was that even with one year as the period for over-all planning, some elements of his business required daily or weekly plans while others required less frequent attention. He recognized, however, that he had to develop a mechanism for making rapid decisions about any aspect of his business and that the development of annual plans helped him create this mechanism. The process of developing the annual (or quarterly) plan for the entire business established procedures for coordinating diverse elements of the business and forced all contributors to raise their sights to at least the horizon of one year.

Until recently, one year was enough for three reasons. First, relatively few activities required thought or coordinated action which took more than a year to prepare for and these activities could be carried out, typically, on an "ad hoc" basis. Second, relatively few commitments of resources would last for more than one year, and third, when they did, they would not be drastically altered by changes taking place during their economic life. Today, all three of these elements have changed. Many more decisions require more than a year to plan for and implement. Second, the size and magnitude of the commitments have implications going much further into the future, and, finally, the future is likely to be less and less like the present and, thus, will have more drastic implications during the life of the commitment.

Add to this the increased complexity involved in making decisions, and it is no wonder that the "ad hoc" approach began to suffer under the strain. As a result, more and more companies have turned to the development of a long-range planning program to try to do on a longer-term basis what annual planning does for shorter-range needs. The biggest single failure in most of these companies has been the failure to recognize that to an even greater degree than in annual planning it is the *process,* the *mechanism* for planning, and *not* the *plan* that is of greatest importance. It cannot be over-emphasized that with few exceptions the purpose of long-range planning is not nearly so much having a plan as developing processes, attitudes, and perspectives which make planning possible. In the ideal, these attitudes and perspectives will aid in the creation of processes which provide a basis for making continuous reappraisals and decisions reflecting the demands of a changing world. Developing formal, comprehensive long-range plans is merely a means to an end. The "plan" itself is likely to be obsolete a week after it is developed. The *process* which created the plan, if carefully conceived, nurtured, and controlled, is not. It is instead the basis for sensing needs and making adjustments continuously. The plan itself is merely a complete and hopefully common point of departure reflecting best guesses about the future which can be used by all areas of the business as a basis for rapidly and economically responding to change. Developing the *plan* ideally should create both the mechanisms and motivations necessary for doing effective *planning.*

Given this view, the choice of a time period for developing formal comprehensive plans becomes relatively unimportant within a range of roughly two to ten years. Obviously, it must go beyond one year and should be long enough to cover most of those decisions which (1) require more than one year to make or (2) commit the company in a major way for more than one year in areas subject to dramatic change. Ten years are selected as an outer limit since relatively few decisions require more than ten years to prepare for and the validity of most key forecasts becomes so low beyond this period as to make them of little value.

Uncertainty and Long-Range Planning

Having considered a number of misconceptions about what long-range planning is, and having offered a definition, the next step is to develop a clear set of realistic expectations for long-range planning. Before this can be done, however, it is necessary to consider the relationship between long-range planning and uncertainty. Time and again in discussions about long-range planning, the reason why executives give little more than lip-service to it is seen to stem from a feeling that because they could not predict the future or influence it in any significant way, they could not do any meaningful longer-range planning. It is easy to sympathize with this position, but it reveals a very basic misconception about the nature and purpose of planning.

Our definition holds that the only valid reasons for engaging in this activity are first to recognize possible implications of long-term commitments made today and to prepare now for commitments which will have to be made rapidly, economically and with a minimum disruption sometime in the future. If the future could be predicted, first the problem of rapid decision making would be reduced, and second, the problems of implementation easily anticipated. The *less* able a company or individual is to predict the future, the *greater* the need for speed and smoothness of implementation. Few major commitments will be made on highly uncertain estimates. The company must wait for greater certainty to act, but to act rapidly as that certainty approaches requires more and better anticipation of what the future *may* be like and the development of plans based on assumptions of perhaps alternative futures. Thus, the company or individual which is least able to predict or influence the future is often the one which needs planning most. To see how misconceptions on the need for more certainty in prediction can sabotage long-range planning, consider this comment by an executive in one of the survey companies where long-range planning practices were studied.

We can estimate what kinds of changes are likely to occur but for the most part we are just guessing. Rather than base our plans on guesses, we assume the future will be largely a continuation of current trends. We know that many of our assumptions will prove incorrect, but so would our guesses. Thus, we base our plans on those things of which we are relatively certain, namely, extrapolation of present trends.

While there are few things which can be predicted with certainty, it is safe to predict that many key elements affecting a business will bear little resemblance to past or even current trends. Yet, the attitude expressed above is not at all uncommon though the candor of the statement may be.

This tendency to shirk from real planning because of the unpredictability of the future is not limited to the difficulty of estimating external, uncontrollable variables. One division director of research and development pointed out that the work of his group in looking for new products and markets was seldom reflected in the division's five-year plan until the product or market had gone through final testing and was ready for introduction. Up to this point only, general comments about the nature of new ventures were included in the introduction to the plan. Such efforts were seen as part of "our continuing search for dynamic means of contributing to corporate growth and profit," but the relationship of this work to forecasted action steps which might be needed to realize this growth and profit were seldom developed far enough in advance to make a rapid, economical, and smooth introduction possible. Again, a basic misconception of the purpose of a forecast is the culprit. While it is seldom easy to arrive at meaningful estimates of the future, it is far better to work with imperfect guesses than with static and unimaginative extrapolations of trend.

A final problem arising from the difficulty in making accurate forecasts is more political than statistical in nature but must be recognized, and attempts must be made to deal with it. A corporate level planning analyst in one of the survey companies made the following observation.

In many cases, . . . [divisional planners] . . . show corporate management what they feel corporate management wants to see. They paint a picture that may be unrealistic, but it normally takes two or three years for this to become apparent. Often they attain their goals for totally different reasons than were planned.

Even more often, as might be expected, they fail to realize their objectives.

Division management seems to take the view that if things don't work out as expected, they have the uncertainty of the future to fall back on. At worst, once every three or four years they may get a real going over, if they haven't already been promoted, but this is accepted as the price paid for freedom to work on the myriad operational problems faced today, rather than tackle more uncertain problems which may be several years away.

Here, the potential planner uses the uncertainty of the future to avoid painting a realistic picture which may damn him for past mistakes or merely bring increased pressure on him sooner to see to it that the future turns out better than he forecast it. Perhaps the underlying cause of all of these misconceptions about the need for dealing with uncertainty in planning is best summed up by a director of market research who complained of his superiors in this way: "They simply do not understand the nature of forecasting. They don't understand the value of working with alternative estimates of the future. They want *answers*."

With their responsibility for making decisions involving thousands, if not millions of dollars, it is not surprising that executives want answers, not estimates. To be sure, they may recognize that a long-range forecast is at best a carefully formulated guess, but it is not really surprising that they should rebel at the idea of receiving these guesses in a form that emphasizes their uncertainty. There seems to be no way to work around this problem. If it is to be met, it must be met head on. One way of doing this is being tried by several companies in which all long-range forecasts of key variables must be developed to reflect what may be expected under "best," "worst," and "most likely" future conditions. Such forecasts reflect the impossibility of precise prediction and lead to the development of plans designed to cope with alternative future conditions.

Basically, much of forecasting is a technical function performed by specialists. The specialists have developed techniques for producing a better basis for forward planning. Great advances have been made in data-processing and developing meaningful measures of subjective probability. But for this progress to have meaning, those who direct the technicians must be prepared to seek and use true forecasts rather than static extrapolations and wish-fulfilling prophecies. As long as executives regard the inability to predict with certainty as an obstacle rather than incentive to forward planning, the activity is doomed to become a relatively meaningless and costly form of self-delusion guaranteed to at least retard effective long-range planning.

A Realistic Set of Expectations

From the position taken here on the nature of long-range planning, a realistic set of expectations is implied. It is, however, worthwhile to look at them briefly in a more explicit form. The major purpose of planning is the development of processes, mechanisms and managerial attitudes which will do two things. First, they will make it possible to make commitment decisions today with a greater awareness of future implications, and second, they will make it possible to make future decisions more rapidly, more economically, and with less disruption to the ongoing business. More specifically, this emphasis on process and attitudes rather than blueprints is directed to accomplishing the following expectations:

Clearer understanding of likely future impacts on present decisions:

First, they should raise the sights of the executive who makes commitment decisions today by bringing a greater degree of awareness of possible changes in the future on decisions involving longer-term commitments. If longer-range planning is successful, the executive who makes and must live with longer-range commitments should feel he is getting more and better data on how a rapidly changing world will affect such commitments. Moreover, he must get such forecasts in a form which reflects the assumptions on which they are based so that they can be tested against his experience and periodically reviewed to test the validity of the forecast.

Anticipating areas requiring future decisions:

Second, the executive should be made more aware, by this process, of key decisions which will have to be made in the future with a fairly clear idea as to when a commitment must be made and in what magnitude. The process should increase his awareness of areas most affected by anticipated changes, both within and outside the firm. It should help him to anticipate likely problem areas and potential profit opportunities which can be minimized on the one hand and maximized on the other by advanced preparation for decisions.

Increasing the speed of relevant information flow:

Third, the executive should feel that the process and changes in attitudes are adding to, and not further complicating and slowing down, the speed and clarity with which information flows among various groups contributing to the planning and decision-making process. The mechanism must not be so complicated and lacking in common language, as is true in many cases today, as to slow down or muddle the flow of relevant data.

Providing for faster and less disruptive implementation of future decisions:

Fourth and finally, the processes and attitudes developed should contribute to the implementation of decisions based on them in a manner which is least disruptive to the organization. If the processes and attitudes do not tend to reduce rather than increase departmental provincialism, they defeat this purpose. Since so many of the key decisions resulting from better long-range planning will have interdepartmental implications, care must be taken to establish an approach which will not reflect increased department bias in the data used to make such decisions. If the participants in this process are convinced that they are contributing to a decision which will be made in a way which is least disruptive to the existing organization, we are well on our way towards realizing this expectation.

Too few companies are obtaining even these benefits from their long-range planning efforts. Their top managements, however, should not be satisfied with anything else.

3

Roadblocks to
Long-Range
Planning

THIS book began with an effort to highlight the need for and value of more and better long-range planning. Because so much has already been written to prove the internal benefits of long-range planning, they received little attention in Chapter 1. Instead, the focus was on the need for better long-range planning in the private sector to (1) maintain our economic position in the face of increased international competition and (2) develop more tenable means of relating private planning to increased governmental participation in the economic sector. Upon reflection, this is quite a powerful one-two punch. One, as a reward for better long-range planning, the executive is promised a better profit picture and fewer headaches (in the long run). Two, he is threatened that if the private sector doesn't do a better job, at best, America's economic position will be weakened and, at worst, the bogey man of government intervention will get him. How can the thoughtful executive fail to respond to these incentives with forceful and timely *action?* Yet, many have failed.

One reason for this failure, discussed in Chapter 2, stems

from confusion about what long-range planning is and what represents, in less global terms than those stated above, a realistic set of expectations for effective planning. Having sought to clarify these issues in Chapter 2, we turn now to three additional roadblocks to translating a felt need for long-range planning into meaningful practices. They are:

1. Often overpowering pressures for present profit.
2. Background and personalities of chief executives and operating personnel.
3. Background and personalities of "staff planners."

Pressure for Present Profits

As noted in Chapter 1, the most common reason given for not doing more or better longer-range planning is lack of time due to present profit pressures. Such planning often comes to be viewed wistfully as a luxury the harried executive would love to indulge himself in if the pressing profit pressures of the present would only permit.

Who cannot afford long-range planning:

It was pointed out in Chapter 1 that since this problem is real it must be faced up to, recognized, and dealt with. For those companies facing heavy profit pressure, the first problem is and must be survival. There is no point in preparing for the future at the expense of the present if this expense is too great. It is perfectly clear that meaningful long-range planning will do nothing to alleviate present profit pressures. In fact, it may very well add to them by draining limited supplies of capital, and most important, the really top executive talent needed to deal with present problems. Companies undergoing extremely tough competition with extremely limited resources, in *most instances*, have no business undertaking long-range planning efforts.

For such companies, efforts must be directed to the present, if necessary, at the expense of the future. It would be nice to know how great the expense is or whether it can be avoided, but the cost of finding out *well may* constitute an outlay such companies *cannot* afford. Long-range planning in such cases may at best dilute their resources and, at worst, it may delude their managements. For such companies, the only longer-range planning which may be appropriate would involve an analysis of possible new products, markets, or mergers which might alleviate profit pressures. This, however, requires sufficient resources to live through what may be a costly period of transition and again may be more than the company can afford.

Companies in this position would do well to devote more time and effort to improving their short-range, day-to-day planning. If they survive, they are then likely to be in a better position to begin longer-range planning. The company which has met pressing problems, not through successful fire fighting but by improving the quality of its short-range planning, is in a much better position subsequently to undertake successful long-range planning efforts. For small companies with very limited resources undergoing heavy profit pressure or the larger companies which are bordering on bankruptcy, however, survival must be paramount and the first steps must be short range.

Who cannot afford not to do long-range planning?

If this seems in conflict with the position taken earlier, it is not since most companies undergoing profit pressure do not fall into this category. There is a great difference between increased profit pressure and cash shortage or imminent bankruptcy. Too many companies, though plagued with pressing problems, have the resources to withstand this pressure, but merely use its tangible nature as a basis for rationalizing poor or inadequate longer-range planning activities. The real causes of unsatisfactory planning in these companies stem from one or both of the remaining roadblocks presented in this chapter.

In support of this position, one need only consider the growing number of companies which, while undergoing profit pressure, are becoming more and more concerned about the fact that their present cash position and anticipated cash flow are and will be in excess of their present and projected business needs. It is not at all uncommon to hear comments such as this:

> While our company has had to face increased pressure from domestic and foreign competition and has seen margins eroded, our big problem is that our forecasted cash flow exceeds our present capacity to utilize it at anything like our present return. Despite competition, we expect to grow at a rate of at least three percent a year but this will barely keep us up with population growth. We must find new markets and new products to utilize these funds!

Summary

In summary, the smaller and relatively vulnerable companies in danger of bankruptcy cannot afford to dilute their resources or delude themselves by doing long-range planning. Only a few will be skillful enough, perhaps, to go through the motions without dilution and internal delusion so as to "impress" stockholders or security analysts sufficiently to gain additional funds to meet their short-range needs. The vulnerable company, however, can profit most by improving its planning skills and organization structure to deal with current problems and in so doing be well on its way to more effective longer-range efforts once past the crisis.

The larger and relatively secure companies, despite profit pressure cannot afford *not* to do longer-range planning. Their long-run survival based on effective use of their resources demands it. While other obstacles remain, the pressures of the present alone must not be used as a basis for rationalizing inadequate longer-range planning.

Background and Personalities of Chief Executive and Operating Personnel

Much of what has been said about pressure for present profits is reflected in the background and personalities of key line executives. It will help, however, to sharpen the focus on this problem by looking more directly at the products of these pressures, today's successful executives.

Attempts to identify the key talents of these men usually have proven most unsatisfactory, because they tend to be overly broad—attributing to the executive every virtue under the sun—or to be too narrow focusing on too few of the elements which lead to his success. One thing is, however, characteristic of every successful executive. He is a man who knows how to make things happen. How they are made to happen will vary not only with the individual but the organization he leads. He is essentially a man of action who typically knows how to use his strengths and complement them to offset his weaknesses. He may be, by nature, reflective and philosophical, but to be successful he has had to learn how to act quickly and decisively or how to attract and live with people who can.

Despite protestations to the contrary, more often than not his activities are dictated by his appointment calendar, his thoughts by the pressures of the day, and his decisions by the form and content of highly summarized recommendations which have been shaped and will be implemented by those below him. A senior executive in a large organization is, and must be, primarily a political leader, in the best sense of the word, who can resolve disputes, inspire confidence, and reduce the burdens of subordinates by accepting ultimate authority for the company's or division's actions. He really formulates few plans, for in most instances the recommendations he receives imply the form of his decisions. Most of his time is spent allocating the power of his office to decisions which are "made" by those below him. This is true to a lesser degree as one descends through the line organization.

He must think ahead, but seldom, as an individual, can he plan ahead in a complete, orderly way which is easily communicable throughout his organization. He may set goals, play a major role in determining broad strategies, and allocate resources, but his organization must translate these acts into plans and programs. Seldom can he afford the luxury of considering all or even most of the possible alternatives or ramifications of the alternative he backs. If this is done, it must and should be done for him in all but a very few cases. Once again, this is true to lesser degrees of his key line subordinates.

Mores and traditions

Historically, this description of key line executives was even more universal then it is today. The great entrepreneurs, while men of vision, were seldom planners. They had new ideas but perhaps more important, they had the talent and toughness to translate ideas into results. These results did not have to be and often were not accomplished in the most efficient way. In an emerging nation, isolated from foreign competition, finding the *best* way was often of secondary importance.

As our industries began to mature by the early 1900's, it became apparent that the companies which would succeed in the face of increasing size would be those which managed to do what they did better, which usually meant more efficiently than their competitors. The entrepreneur began to give way to the professional manager. Frederick Taylor and other proponents of scientific management came to the fore. The passing of the first federal income tax laws, and later laws governing financial reporting for publicly held companies, laid the groundwork for more short range, financial planning by forcing an orderly approach to record keeping.

By the late thirties, executives had not only developed an awareness of the need for better short-range planning to meet competition but had developed techniques for doing such planning. Most of the men now holding key executive positions are products of this transitionary period or were shaped and seasoned by men who were.

The executive today

While the top executive accepts the need for more short-range planning, quite often it is begrudgingly, damning the red-tape and details which size, complexity, and competition have made necessary. More often than not, they delegate it to the specialists, the accountants, the time-and-motion men, and more recently, the market researchers. This is possible, because the techniques for doing such short-range planning and budgeting, as well as the activities planned, have become more precise over the years and the results of such efforts can be summarized and acted on.

This somewhat lengthy digression into an exploration of factors influencing the attitudes of many of today's successful executives is vital to an understanding of their attitudes toward new pressures to do more formalized long-range planning. Historically, they have been users of plans, not planners. They have tolerated planning as a necessary evil in a world experiencing increased growth in both institutions and competition. It was, however, a world which by today's standards was changing quite slowly and in a much less complex way. Today, they must use plans and planners of a very different type and make up. Unlike a production schedule or quarterly budget, long-range plans must deal not only with a much higher degree of uncertainty but be geared to an ever accelerating rate of change.

Given these conditions, it is not hard to understand why so many executives have accepted the need for more long-range planning but have not gotten far in translating this need into action. Presently accepted and implemented short-range planning techniques succeeded not only because the need for them was great and the executive soon learned their limits and place in management, but because three additional factors held true. Namely:

1. The technicians who developed and carried them out were able to deal effectively over an extended time with the executives who had to use them.
2. The techniques were refined to a point where the executive's ability to understand and have confidence in them increased.
3. Since the techniques dealt essentially with more tangible short-range issues, the executive using them had the capacity to measure their effectiveness in relatively clear terms before too much time had elapsed.

Given the success with short-range planning, it is not surprising to see executives attempt to use it as a substitute for long-range planning in the form of crash programs. To see how this approach goes, consider the following statement by a vice president of marketing of a large electronics firm:

> Suppose a well planned program would require two years work and the efforts of five key men. If we miss the boat and find we only have a year to get the program launched, we simply put ten key men to work on it. More often than not, because they are running scared, they can get it done in less than a year.

While this approach may work at times, there are essentially two problems with it. First, there is doubt as to whether over an extended time people perform better when "running scared," and even if executives are working effectively, a crash program is normally a rather costly substitute for effective longer-range planning. At a time when domestic and international competition are increasing the profit squeeze even during a period of expansion, the crash program is rapidly becoming an even greater luxury than planning.

The second problem with crash programs, and this has always been true, stems from the fact that some projects simply cannot be telescoped. As Michael Kami, director of long-range planning at Xerox points out, "Making nine women pregnant will not produce a baby in one month." Similarly, putting nine research and development people to work on a new product may not produce that product in one month. Quite often, multiplying the number of people and resources needed to bring off a crash program merely increases the difficulty of the task by multiplying and complicating communication and co-ordination problems. More and more today, the kind of projects which contribute to long-range success depend on factors such as research or personnel development which resist telescoping. Finally, the increasing size and complexity of the modern corporation makes the implementation of a crash program considerably more disruptive.

Summary

While the background and personality of chief executives and operating personnel may present a formidable roadblock to long-range planning, there is equal danger of it producing acute cases of managerial schizophrenia. The same executive, shaped by his background and successful in the past by virtue of his action-oriented personality who feels the need for more long-range planning, also feels the tugs which prevent him from being able to get it done. As a result, perhaps to maintain his sanity, he often delegates key responsibilities in the planning area to staff personnel. This delegation, a source of potential help, within the survey companies has often backfired. To see why, it is necessary to consider the background and personalities of typical "staff planners."

Background and Personalities of "Staff Planners"

At a recent American Management Association meeting it was reported that more than 700 U.S. companies had one or more employees with the title "planner." The report went on to point out that in 500 of these 700 companies the planners have been hired in the last five years. Two questions come to mind immediately. What do these "planners" do and what types of talents and temperaments do they bring to bear on their tasks?

From the discussion in Chapter 2, it would seem that some of the men AMA calls corporate planners are in a sense the valuable technicians who carry out or make major contributions to the activities described in Chapter 2 and summarized below:

1. Preparing forecasts of events likely to have an impact on elements of the business.

2. Analyzing results to identify potential trouble spots and opportunities.

3. Collecting data to serve as a basis for making key assumptions.

4. Formulating and analyzing alternative action programs.

5. Translating these programs into financial terms and preparing necessary support data.

The problems faced by men performing these elements of long-range planning in their dealings with line executives, on the surface, are neither new nor radically different from the problems encountered in short-range, day-to-day planning. They have their parallels in the military where the need for acting quickly as an integrated whole led to the creation of staff-line concepts. For the most part, our companies have done a fairly good job of merging the different talents and temperaments found in staff and line managers. Where the line executive tends to be more intuitive and empirical, the staff man will tend to be more scientific and theoretical. The line executive's intolerance of ambiguity is set against the staff man's attempts to find concepts which resolve ambiguity through higher-order abstraction. Numerous books and articles have dealt with these generalized differences and the implications they have on relationships between staff and line. We will focus here only on the degree to which these problems are intensified when the staff-line conflicts center around long-range planning.

In comparison to longer-range planning, staff-line conflicts are minimized in short-range planning, because the issues dealt with are more tangible, and the results will shortly, and in tangible terms, reassure the line executive of the value of staff advice or give him the ammunition he needs to change his staff. Similarly, staff personnel are able to confirm or modify their judgments on line personnel based on rapid settlement of disputes by fairly tangible short-range results.

The more intangible the issues, the more uncertain the premises, the more long-run and intangible the results, the greater the potential conflict in the personalities and tasks of line and staff executives. Thus, the key to minimizing this conflict between staff and line lies in increasing the tangibility and reliability of long-range planning and by improving techniques for measuring the planning effort rather than its results. Accomplishing these ends is so vital that the next three chapters of this book are devoted to them.

The director of long-range planning: The nature of the job

In addition to the technicians who carry out much of the data collection, analysis, and program development involved in planning, many companies in recent years have appointed someone to a position which is typically called vice-president or director of long-range planning. Unlike the technicians who may work for him or in other staff or line departments, the men who bear the title director of planning typically make very little direct contribution to the development of plans. Where they do, in most cases, they should not. Where they have been used most successfully, they have been regarded primarily as architects and overseers whose major task is the development of a sound planning process rather than actual planning. In addition, it falls on them to help reshape line executives' attitudes toward long-range planning and create an environment in which to minimize the potentially negative impact of the first two roadblocks considered in this chapter. At least these are the tasks to which they should devote most of their talents. Unfortunately, as a result of misconceptions about the nature and purposes of long-range planning, they are often selected with other ideas in mind or soon find themselves carrying out other duties.

Although the chief executive or his key line subordinates might be thought of as having the major responsibility for designing, selling, and directing a long-range planning effort, this is not typically the case. In most of the companies studied, the line executives confine their direct efforts to rather broad and summary analysis and review. They give direction by decision, administer by reaction and coordinate and sell by arbitration. With the exception of setting broad company goals, premises and constraints, they are essentially reactors rather than active participants in these areas of planning. Given other tasks which they must perform, this is probably a sensible approach, but it requires that the men who are to play a more direct role in the design and administration of the planning process be selected with a clear notion of the intellectual and political difficulties they must be equipped to face.

The ideal choice for such a post should be a man who is both philosopher and realist, theoretician and practical politician, soothsayer and salesman and, as one planner points out, he probably should be able to walk on water. A few companies have succeeded in finding men who possess some of these talents and they have done so because they made their selections realizing the job to be done and the talents and temperaments required. More often, because of misconceptions about the nature and purpose of planning, men selected for this key job have been poor ones.

If long-range planning is confused with one of its major parts or elements, such as forecasting or budgeting, the job may be filled with someone who is a first-rate marketing research director or controller but who lacks the conceptual and/or political skills needed to design, sell, and administer an effective long-range planning process. While there have been notable exceptions because the man selected had talents which went beyond the requirements of his previous functional specialties, more often than not this happy choice was accidental.

The controller as director of long-range planning

Until recently, most of the men selected for this post were former controllers—and at times, they were asked to perform the almost impossible task of serving as controller and as director of long-range planning. The task is viewed as impossible, because of more or less basic conflicts between need for the controller to be guardian of corporate resources or, as he is often seen, to be "the president's all seeing eye," and the need for a planning designer who can gain the confidence of line and staff participants in planning. Some controllers sought to overcome this by delegating to a subordinate the task of designing and administering a plan for planning. By so doing, however, they often diluted one of the major reasons for their initial selection. That is, the political power and prestige of their office.

The major reason for selecting the controller, beyond his power as holder of the purse strings, stemmed from the misconception that since all plans must eventually be translated into financial terms, the controller would be a logical choice. To so equate planning and budgeting is like asking the director of that hard-working group of technicians at the United Nations who translate speeches and policy statements from one language to another to play a major role in writing speeches and policy statements. The analogy holds in that while the control and budgeting function is one of the most vital activities in a company, it is essentially oriented toward translation from the language of ideas and objectives into the language of dollars and cents.

While this certainly is not true of all who rise from the controller's ranks, the individual who at least historically was most successful as a controller achieved his success because he possessed talents and attitudes which are almost antithetical to those required in a director of long-range planning. A strong statement on this point was offered by a former member of the corporate planning staff of one of the survey companies. He said:

> The controller's main job is to see that the resources of the business are conserved and being used efficiently. In accomplishing this task he uses the tools of accounting, auditing, and more recently, budgeting and forecasting. Because of his interest in conservation and efficiency, the controller normally has a functional bias in the direction of saving rather than spending money. His work is primarily with figures and, of necessity, is oriented toward recording and examining the results of past operations. His task is to measure the results of risks taken by other functions of the business rather than to take risks himself. . . . Within such a setting, it is only to be expected that forecasting, as de-

veloped by the controller, has tended to be a projection of past trends into the future.

Long-range planning, on the other hand, must contend with the risks of innovation and deal with the exceptional and improbable future. It must be concerned with risk-taking—spending money to make money. The measure of the effectiveness of long-range planning is not efficiency but how well the course of business has been charted on the sea of future risk. Above all, those entrusted with the responsibility for long-range planning must be oriented toward the future—not the past. They must be able to take risk in their stride—not pass the risk to others or act as a passive observer or measurer. The long-range planner must lead—not follow. . . .

Placing the long-range planning function under the average controller will assure its sterility.

While this may overstate the case, particularly in light of efforts in recent years by such top-flight organizations as the Financial Executives' Institute, the viewpoint still has substantial validity.

Other choices for director of long-range planning

Confusion between long-range planning and one of its major parts or elements contributes to the selection of men who, while they possess great ability in some technical area, lack the other requirements for carrying out this demanding job. In addition, confusing long-range planning with one of the key areas in which it is required can lead to other types of problems. Thus, if long-range planning is regarded as synonymous with new-product planning or merger and acquisition planning, the man selected as director of planning is likely to be chosen because of his talents in one of these areas. This is less undesirable than errors leading to the selection of a man who has experience in but one phase of planning, such as forecasting or budgeting. While some longer-range planning will emerge, it is likely to be limited to one or two areas. If, instead, the company seriously seeks to develop methods and attitudes which will foster better planning in all phases of its business, it is unlikely to get these results directly.

Some companies have wisely limited their experience in formalized long-range planning to one key area, such as new-product development. They have sought to use this approach as an experiment to learn what more comprehensive planning will require and to chalk up some tangible results in the new product area to use as selling points in subsequent larger scale planning programs. If this approach is taken, however, it should be understood clearly at the outset that more limited objectives are being sought. More than one long-range planning program has failed because the director of long-range planning was selected with one specific aspect of planning in mind and then subsequently expected to design a mechanism for more comprehensive planning.

A poor choice for the post of director of planning which was based on confusion between planning and one of its elements (e.g. forecasting) or one of its key areas (e.g. new-product planning) may be serious, but it is not likely to be nearly as disastrous as the following choices. In some companies men appointed to this job have been selected not because they possessed the necessary talents, but because they had the potential for some other job, and, as director of planning, they would gain valuable experience. In most cases, such a choice is doomed to failure unless the planning process is well established and accepted. It is most dangerous to mix executive development with an attempt to get this vital and often misunderstood activity off the ground.

Another unfortunate choice is the appointment of a man who is regarded as an "ivory tower" theorist. He possesses all of the technical skills necessary to design a theoretically sound process but lacks either the necessary knowledge of the business or the political skills, or both, to fit this process to the needs and requirements of those who contribute to and use the plans which should result. Such a man, however, may be a most valuable member of the director's staff, if the director can complement his skills with the practical and political know-how which is needed.

Along the same general lines has been a tendency in some companies to select for this position a man who has been a capable line executive but who has been "booted upstairs" for one reason or another. Too often such a man, in an effort to prove to himself, if not others, that he still has what it takes to carry line responsibility will play too active a role in the development of plans. As a result, he will tend to hinder the development and acceptance of the planning *process* which is sought.

Finally, a few appointments to this post have been men who are generally regarded as corporate misfits. Extremely bright, if not brilliant, they are potentially too capable to fire, but no one knows quite where or how to use them. Undoubtedly, there is a place for such men, but director of planning hardly seems a good choice. When such a man is selected, it is usually a fairly clear indication of corporate management's failure to understand the nature of long-range planning or accept its importance.

Summary

By exploring in this chapter three major roadblocks to effective planning, the first step to reducing, if not removing, them has been taken. Few serious problems have been solved without first seeking to understand their nature, origin and impact. Having done this, we turn in the remaining chapters to a look at why these roadblocks have not been removed or detoured and what is required to do the job.

4

Response of Operating Executives to Long-Range Planning Efforts

W_{HILE} the obstacles to effective long-range planning discussed in Chapter 3 are serious, they can and, in time, will be removed. How long it takes will be largely a function of the amount and caliber of top management talent devoted to the task. Currently, far too little top talent is being devoted, and the reason goes to the heart of what might be described as management's schizophrenic attitude toward planning.

Measurement and Control: The Missing Link

True management talent is undoubtedly the scarcest resource in a corporation. The chief executive, despite his intuitive feel for the value of any activity, is justifiably slow to commit such a scarce resource without an adequate measure of payoff. Regardless of the inherent importance of long-range planning, *inability to measure the payoff* has led the executives of most of the survey companies to hedge their bets and, in far too many instances, dilute the efforts of those who seek to remove the obstacles to effective long-range planning.

The purpose of this and the next two chapters will be to examine the following three questions.

1. How do operating executives respond to typical long-range planning efforts, given the absence of effective measurement and control? (Chapter 4)

2. How are long-range planning efforts being measured and evaluated at present, and what is wrong with these approaches? (Chapter 5)

3. What constitutes a better approach to the problem? (Chapter 6)

How the Absence of Effective Measurement Undermines Long-Range Planning

Where effective techniques for measuring an activity exist and are used, those involved in carrying out the activity recognize that success or failure on their part is likely to be detected, and they will be rewarded or penalized accordingly. As a result, given limited time and resources, managers will logically allocate more of both to those activities which can be accurately measured. In the absence of effective evaluation techniques, two other factors determine the way these resources are allocated. They are:

1. The individual manager's personal interest and commitment to the activity.

2. The willingness of high levels of management to devote their time and resources to the activity and place pressure on lower levels despite the absence of better evaluation techniques.

Since lower levels of management are likely to find long-range planning a far more difficult area in which to work and since they are aware of the tangible measures used in evaluating short term performance, personal commitment and interest at lower levels tend to be slight. Therefore, if lower levels of management are to devote time and talent to long-range planning in the absence of sound evaluation, usually it will be as a result of the second factor noted above. This could be seen throughout the survey companies. Lacking direct feedback from higher levels, lower levels of management would "test" top level commitment to planning in several ways. The "testing" begins almost immediately after a new activity, not subject to effective control, is introduced.

To see how the absence of effective measurement undermines long-range planning is to see how top management meets, or more accurately, fails to meet these tests. It begins with the introduction of formalized long-range planning to the divisions. This introduction was usually heralded in the survey companies by a memorandum from the president to corporate level executives who upon receipt would add a few words of personal endorsement and send the memorandum on down the line. A typical statement to be found in such presidential memoranda is the following:

> Given the ever increasing complexity of our business and the continuing profit pressure, it is my opinion that our future success will be in large part dependent on our ability to develop a better, more comprehensive approach to long-range planning. As a result, I am appointing Mr. _____ _____ as corporate director of long-range planning, reporting to _____ _____.
>
> While Mr. _____ _____ will have primary responsibility for developing a mechanism for facilitating and coordinating our company's total planning effort, it should be understood that in this era of dynamic competition and accelerating change, long-range planning has become an increasingly important part of every manager's responsibility.
>
> Mr. _____ _____ has not only my complete support in carrying out his new duties, but I am sure he will receive the cooperation he needs throughout the organization.

The experienced executive receiving such a memorandum adds it to a file which might be labeled "Wait-and-See." In this file he has a number of memoranda which sound remarkably like the latest. In fact, he might substitute "market research" or "systems analysis" for "long-range planning," and the three most recent additions will sound almost identical.

The wise president knows that no "new" activity like formal, long-range planning will get off the ground without his "whole hearted support and undivided attention." Similarly, wise subordinates realize that it is impossible for the chief executive to give "whole hearted support and undivided attention" to all of the things which come out over his signature. And so, they adopt a wait-and-see attitude, unless by chance the memo deals with one of their pet projects or strong interests.

Testing the Importance of Long-Range Planning

During the wait-and-see period, lower levels begin to test the president's intent. If he had effective measures to evaluate their efforts in this area, his response to the measures would be the best test. In the absence of such measures, four more indirect tests typically are used.

Test 1: Who is chosen as planning director and how is he treated by top management?

The first test begins with a careful appraisal of the man chosen as director or coordinator of planning. What is his background? Is this a promotion or demotion for him? Whom does he report to? What kind of real support will he get from the top? These are only some of the questions which, however imperfectly answered, will play a key role in lower level appraisals of the new activity's importance. While the choice of men to fill these key posts was considered briefly in Chapter 3, the impact of this choice on the response of operating people to long-range planning deserves additional consideration here.

As pointed out in Chapter 3, because of misconceptions about what long-range planning is and what should be expected from it, some men are appointed to this key post who lack the blend of talent, temperament, and political savvy which the job requires. To both corporate and divisional personnel, such an unfortunate appointment may trigger either or both of the following responses. First, to the degree that the managers who "appraise" the new appointee decide he is ill equipped for the job, they tend either to discount the true importance placed on the activity by the president or to feel that any errors made by *them* in the area of long-range planning can easily be ascribed to the appointee's deficiencies.

A second and often more common reaction by corporate and divisional personnel working with the new appointee is to define what long-range planning means and what should be expected in terms of *his* talents and interests. This response might be characterized as "If this is who the president put in charge, then it's obvious that what he will expect is . . ." Thus, a poor selection for the key post tends to slant the direction and narrow the importance of long-range planning at the outset. In several of the survey companies, however, a truly first rate individual was selected for the post of planning director or coordinator. In these instances, the question of whom he reported to and how much influence he wielded became important in determining how much weight to give to the presidential memorandum. If he measured up well by these criteria and is viewed as not only capable but someone who could be of help and who wielded considerable influence, the planning function usually gets off to a good start. In several of the survey companies, however, this "good start" led to unexpected and somewhat paradoxical problems.

In at least two instances, the successes of the new directors of planning were interpreted by their presidents and top executive groups as evidence that their companies had found in these individuals men who were far too capable to waste on opportunities five or more years ahead when the companies had so many challenging projects which could utilize their skills and which demanded immediate action. The planners in question were both flattered by this recognition and at the same time saw no way to turn down what their presidents felt was an "unparalleled opportunity."

In one instance, the former director of planning accepted a post as general manager of a new division that had been created largely through his efforts. It would be poetic justice to learn that as a line executive this very capable staff man had failed, but "unfortunately" this didn't happen. The man in question appears to be as capable a line executive as he was a top staff planner.

In the other case, the successful director of planning became a special assistant to the president acting as his personal trouble shooter and doing most of the company's merger and acquisition studies. He too has been quite successful in his new post and the reader may reasonably ask "What's wrong?" These sound like two instances where corporations have profited by having long-range planning. True, but ironically only in the *short run*.

In both of the situations described above, the men who replaced their successful predecessors turned out to be much less capable of developing a sound mechanism for getting integrated long-range planning done. The key line and staff personnel with whom they had to work became quite guarded in their dealings with them for a variety of reasons. The two most prominent were, first, no one was quite sure where the planning director might be in a few more years or what power he might wield. Second, many feared that since the post of director of planning seemed to be a stepping stone, they were leery of the new men turning out to be opportunists who would seek to make a splash at their expense. At the same time, neither of the new men had the same degree of interest or commitment to developing a sound approach to long-range planning. They also viewed their new posts, based on their predecessors' progress, as a final training and testing ground before, hopefully, bigger and better things. The new directors of planning, seeing themselves as in a fishbowl, took few real chances and tended, paradoxically, to do everything possible to make long-range planning "successful" in the short run.

On the other hand, the line and staff personnel whose involvement and continuing cooperation are vital to success in this area got two "messages" loud and clear:

1. We generally do not put our top talent to work on long-range planning, but if we find we have a really capable person in the post we will yank him fast and put him to work where his talents will show up in faster and more tangible returns.

2. Watch out for the person in this post, for if he sees an opportunity to follow his predecessor up the ladder he may use your necks for rungs.

There is nothing *wrong* with this if the key post of planning director is to be viewed only as an executive finishing school. There are, however, many other ways to put potential top level executives through final grooming and testing which do not have such great costs. The selection of top talent for the job of director of planning is important, but equally important, to avoid undermining the activity, is a willingness to (1) leave the capable man on the job and (2) appraise him and reward him for his contributions to the long-run betterment of the company, not glamourous short-run results.

Test 2: How much direct backing does the president give longer-range proposals?

While the selection and handling of the director of corporate planning is one of the first tests for determining how seriously to take the memorandum on long-range planning, the second test is even more important. This second test was most clearly stated by a department manager in one survey company. He said:

Before I take a chance of making my current results look somewhat worse by spending more time and money on the longer run, I want some evidence that the higher echelons are willing to do the same thing at their levels.

For the first three years we got at least one pep talk a month on long-range planning. We were required to develop detailed five-year plans and ten-year forecasts, but every time we submitted a proposal designed to strengthen our company's future position, all we would hear was "how much do we get next year?" They finally approved one project which was recognized as primarily a prestige operation which would, over the next five or ten years, show no direct profit but which would indirectly benefit the entire company. Yet when the operation ran into the red for two years, as projected in the plan, top management demanded that it be put on a profitable basis. We have done so, but the prestige and long-term benefits went down the drain.

In another of the survey companies a project manager echoed this sentiment when he related the following story:

In one of the first years we had a go at formal long-range planning, two months after the five-year plan had been approved, the president announced that all division budgets were to be cut by a flat 3 per cent. Of course, the longer-range projects were the first to be abandoned and the general feeling was that long-range planning is important—when you can afford it. This is one hell of an attitude in a company which has a strong capital position and where for years division management has been encouraged to find ways of using available capital. The only reason given for the cut was that it was necessary to bring that year's expenditures into line with anticipated revenue. We were in a strong cash position and could have easily financed future growth with past earnings, but this was deemed "fiscal irresponsibility."

There are companies whose capital position is so precarious as to make a cautious budgeting policy necessary and to place a premium on keeping annual outlays below anticipated income. Unfortunately for these companies their long-run improvement is usually dependent on a willingness to spend now for future results. What is more disturbing than companies which find themselves in a damned-if-I-do, damned-if-I-don't position, however, are companies, like the one described in the last example, that enjoy a favorable capital position and still view the occasional periods of "deficit financing" as fiscal irresponsibility.

In several cases, the pressure for short-term payoff despite encouragement for more long-range planning took on a somewhat more subtle form. Corporate management spoke out for new ideas, and planning for the future, but each plan requiring long-term capital investment would be subjected to such arbitrary, short-term yardsticks as "payback period" which only measure how fast the investment is returned. To several members of the corporate budget and analysis groups, where these criteria were applied, the fact that these yardsticks were almost automatic rejections of longer-range thinking seemed to be overlooked. In questioning the director of one such corporate budget and analysis group on the investment criteria used, he smiled and said, "Aren't we getting off the subject of long-range planning?" This man was in fact one of the brightest, most alert men interviewed and appeared to be doing a good job in pulling together division five-year plans. Yet, the connection between investment criteria and long-range planning seemed to him at least obscure.

In a number of instances, the question was raised as to whether a yardstick such as "discounted cash flow" might not be more appropriate for long-range proposals, since this method is designed to reflect the relative value of programs over time. The most common response was that this technique was too difficult for division and lower levels of management to understand. In two cases, the interviewer learned that this technique is used by corporate management on borderline cases but "We don't go into this with the divisions, because it is too complicated. In fact, we seldom tell them when this technique is used for fear it will confuse them."

It would seem that the necessary effort to educate division personnel to the ways of "cash flow" analysis or at least encouraging them to take a longer-term view by indicating that their long-range plans are being evaluated on the basis of long-range standards is a vital part of making long-range planning an accepted divisional activity. For divisions to be upset by the use of such a yardstick only serves to prove that division management does not wish to be judged on a long-term basis. It is difficult to imagine any division taking long range planning very seriously when their efforts in this area, including requests for capital to meet a long-range program, must be justified by such short-term yardsticks as the payback approach.

A third and quite direct basis used by managers at all levels for determining what the president means by long-range planning and how much real support he will give to the activity is his (and his supporting review groups') response to both strong and weak long-range planning efforts. Again, before risking their short-term performance pictures by spending time and resources on longer-range problems, most executives look for indications of what happens when someone presents a poorly conceived plan but excellent operating performance for corporate review. Conversely, they will be equally interested in what happens when someone presents a long-range plan which reflects real effort, sound thinking, and great promise, but where he has shown somewhat unsatisfactory short-term performance. No one expects the man with good results and poor plans to be fired but will he be pushed to explain how much of his current success is based on potential shortsightedness? Will he be required to revise his "plans" or at least devote more effort to them?

Similarly, no reasonable person expects the manager who shows an unsatisfactory short-term picture to be given a whopping bonus because he has done a good job of planning. But will management seek to determine how much of the short-term trouble is a result of *necessary first steps* toward a sounder long-term picture? Will he be pushed to determine whether the short-term picture could be improved by sounder, tougher management but not pushed to use means which are likely to be *more* detrimental in the long run?

One corporate planning analyst, referred to in Chapter 2, criticized the quality of many of the five-year programs he received. His chief criticism was that they simply were not realistic. He went on to say that often the objectives set represent little more than wishful thinking, because they are based on unrealistic forecasts. Moreover, the programs which were supposed to be the basis for achieving these objectives were little more than broadly worked out sub-goals rather than more specific series of action steps. Because of this rather severe criticism, he was asked what corporate management did in response to such poor planning. His answer, later supported by interviews with other corporate staff personnel, was:

> Until quite recently, the majority of our operating committee [the group which passed final judgment on division plans] did not really seem interested in the realism of division objectives or the skill and imagination reflected in the design of programs developed for their fulfillment. All they wanted to see were the financial implications of the projected programs. If the numbers came out all right, then the thought and action which should have been the basis for these numbers were presumed to be all right.
>
> At times [he said] I thought that this company was run under the principles of "financial Calvinism"—hard work plus good ideals and balanced books equals success and corporate redemption.

He went on to note that division management was aware of this corporate philosophy and planned accordingly. Periodically, results would clearly indicate that real planning work had not been done and a few heads would roll, but time and changing conditions had a way of camouflaging results so as to make their causes difficult to isolate.

The opinion of both corporate and some divisional personnel interviewed in this company was that unless corporate management took a stronger stand against poor *plans* rather than poor *results*, then divisional personnel could rightfully assume that it was simply the quality of results and not the quality of plans that mattered. This would, in turn, be interpreted as a tacit approval of the use of short-term "fire-fighting" techniques as long as they produced good results.

Test 4: How much emphasis is given to long-range planning in determining bonuses, promotions, etc.?

While the astute manager is interested in the verbal response of top management to strong and weak attempts at long-range planning, he is far more interested in seeing who is promoted, and where the biggest bonuses and salary increases go. This is the acid test.

Time and again within the survey companies, cynicism toward the importance of long-range planning was based on what managers saw as repeated evidence that promotions, bonuses, and salary increases were earned almost entirely on the basis of short-term results, despite verbal insistence that long- and short-range efforts were considered. If the results were good, whether they had been achieved because of sound long-range planning or by wild, last-minute scrambling seemed relatively unimportant. Despite the fact that this tended to reduce the time and talent devoted to long-range planning at almost all levels of management, many of the top officers of the survey companies accepted this as a necessary fact of corporate life. As one executive vice president put it, "It has to be *results* that count. It always has been and always will."

Strangely, he said it as though he expected an argument. When the interviewer agreed, he seemed disturbed and went on, "We demand attention to long-range planning but not as an end in itself. Thus, we measure the quality of the planning the same as we measure anything else: by the results it produces."

At this point the interviewer asked, "How can you tell whether current success has been achieved at the expense of the future?"

His reply was, "If a man takes action which will make him look good today at the expense of tomorrow, then tomorrow he will have to face the music."

The difficulty is that tomorrow the company "will face the music," but whether the misfortunes can be traced to a particular person's shortsightedness three to five years earlier is a gamble many line officers are willing to take rather than face the far more certain disaster that would accompany poor results for the current operating period.

Summary

The dangers of using this "management-by-results" approach to evaluate long-range planning leads us to the second key question: how are long-range planning efforts being measured and evaluated at present and what is wrong with these approaches? Chapter 5 is directed toward answering this question and Chapter 6 will seek to answer the next question: what constitutes a sound approach to measuring and controlling formalized long-range planning?

5

Measurement and Control:

Why Present

Practices Fail

As SEEN in Chapter 4, if an effective approach to measuring and controlling long-range planning is not developed, lower levels of management seek to test higher management's interest in the activity in a number of indirect ways. Unfortunately, within the survey companies, top management all too often fails to pass these "tests." As a result, the response at lower levels to verbal pressure for improved long-range planning has been verbal acceptance but little effective effort.

Before attempting, in Chapter 6, to develop a sounder approach to measurement and control in this area, we must first consider in some detail the nature of present measurement and control devices and their effectiveness and shortcomings with respect to formalized long-range planning.

The Management-by-Results Approach

Far and away, the most commonly used device within the survey companies is the management-by-results approach. In his landmark book, *Management by Results* [1], Edward Schleh described the origin of management by results as an outgrowth of the dilemma which faced managers who were attempting to coordinate and control business organizations of ever increasing size and complexity. Schleh points out that in order to control the "sprawling, expensive and complicated industrial machine" which evolved in the last fifty years and continues to grow in both size and complexity, "budgets . . . [seemed] . . . to be the natural answer. By reviewing a mass of figures, a top manager . . . [may feel] . . . he has control, forgetting that figures in and of themselves do not control men, their ambitions, their drives, their initiative, or the exercise of their judgment." [2]

The response at lower levels to this form of centralized, largely financial control Schleh sees as one of growing discontent, apathy, and conformity. He sees lower level management, conditioned by ever expanding aspirations rising from our political and social system, becoming more and more frustrated with centralized control and attempts to routinize work in accord with the principles of Frederick Taylor's concepts of scientific management. Higher levels of management sense this apathy and conformity and, in turn, are frustrated by what they see as lack of imagination and willingness to accept responsibility at lower levels. Schleh implies that top management failed for years to realize that a major cause of these undesirable attitudes was the kind of control system they had created. Instead, they saw increased apathy and irresponsibility as a call for still tighter and more centralized controls, and the vicious cycle would begin another and broader sweep. To Schleh and others like Harold Smiddy, formerly of General Electric, the only way out lay in top management reversing the process and instituting greater decentralization and management by results. Lower levels would be counselled on what would be expected of them, in terms of over-all results, and

---

[1] E. C. Schleh, *Management by Results* (New York: McGraw-Hill, 1961).

[2] *Ibid.*, p. 4.

then given much greater freedom to determine how these results are to be achieved.

Movement toward this form of decentralized organization
became almost a full-blown fad during the early 1950's. The
chief executive officer of one of the survey companies, a pio-
neer in the decentralization movement, argued that what he
had done with respect to lower levels of management within
his company mirrored what any good board of directors does
for top level management. The good board, after carefully reviewing the over-all performance of the top executive group
and its broad objectives for the future, wisely delegates to that
group the responsibility for determining the details of how
these objectives are to be realized. In turn, he felt he could
best develop a sense of true entrepreneurial responsibility in
subordinates by following much the same procedure that his
board followed with him. For top management to push too
deeply into the affairs of its divisions bred irresponsibility on
the part of division managers. Thus, in this company the term
"staff" was abolished. Corporate "service" groups were created
to assist the divisions but, for the most part, only if the divisions requested the assistance. Wherever possible, this concept
was pushed further down the line to the sub-sections of the
divisions. Each manager was asked to think of himself as the
"president" of a smaller business within the total company.
Given this approach, it was not really surprising to have been
told by an executive in this company, as noted earlier, "It has
to be results that count . . . We demand attention to long-
range planning, but not as an end in itself. Thus, we measure
the quality of planning the same as we measure anything else;
by the results it produces."

Whatever the benefits to be realized from decentralization
and/or management by results, two serious problems arise
when this approach is followed with respect to long-range
planning. They evolve from:

1. The tendency for "results" to become synonymous with *profit*
or tangible short-run results.

2. The relatively short tenure for most executives in middle and upper middle management positions.

Let us consider both in some detail.

**Conflicts between management by
results and long-range planning**

For management by results to succeed in producing sound long-range as well as short-range plans, a class of results must be found which acts as an accurate indicator of the future. Normally, a result tells what has happened. Results such as profit and rate of return, while of vital interest to management, are in general less than satisfactory indicators of what will happen. Whether a good profit picture, based on results, will lead to a good profit picture in the future depends on the *means* employed in reaching this profit and the steps which are anticipated for the future.

Thus, we must look for results which by their nature are indicative of future success. Schleh recognizes this need and emphasizes that "specific results expected must be designed so that they encourage the man on the job to blend short-range into long-range." [3] But how is this to be done? Schleh suggests that, for salesmen, insistence on good results in getting a certain number of new accounts and a certain percentage of sales for new products must be made as important as results in terms of established customers and products. Similarly, setting maintenance results for production will move toward the same objective.

These are, however, merely faltering first steps when applied to long-range plans rather than intangible elements of short-range plans and even they may be ignored in favor of the more pressing short-term results. Consider the following account related by a division manager in a large chemical company. He pointed out that his sales manager, on one occasion,

---

[3] Schleh, p. 4.

had laid off three missionary salesmen to reduce costs for the last quarter of a given year so as to meet his budgeted profit goals. He knew that replacements for these three men would be needed in the spring as business increased, and it was estimated that the cost of finding, screening, and training new men was considerably higher than the payroll cost involved in keeping the three men. Although in principle he disapproved of the action, the division manager permitted it for the following reasons: (1) the year's profit objective would be met, (2) the firing and subsequent hiring would not be revealed in the summary data he presented to top management; and (3) because the profit goal had been met there would be no problem getting approval for sufficient funds in next year's budget to rehire three salesmen.

The division manager commented that he was competing with more than sixteen other divisions for recognition and funds and based on his experience his division would, he felt, be better off in the "long run" if he showed a solid profit picture for the year. Such a picture, in his opinion, was the only way to get the funds he required to "continue the work needed to build the long-run success of my division."

A subsequent analysis of the division's performance, however, showed a history of repeated short-run oriented behavior, such as that noted above. The more support and funds this manager received, the more he felt the need to do an even better job *next year*, more often than not, at the expense of the future. How long he could have kept on "mortgaging the future" became an academic question for him as his "excellent results" led to his promotion. His successor was the man who had to "face the music."

Ironically, the president of the company in question was among the most outspoken proponents of creating key results in areas which focus on factors other than profitability. He was not alone. The president of another survey company was quoted as saying that while traditional measures, such as profit, return on investment, turnover, and percent of earnings to sales, provide useful information ". . . they are hopelessly inadequate as measures to guide the manager's effectiveness in planning for the future of the business—the areas where his decisions have the most important effects."

Seeking to Modify the Approach

This president, with the help of one of the nation's foremost consultants and management thinkers, created the following eight "key result areas" which were designed to provide for balance at lower levels. They are:

1. Profitability
2. Market position
3. Productivity, or the effective integration of human, capital, and material resources
4. Product leadership
5. Personnel development
6. Employee attitudes
7. Public responsibility
8. Balance between short-range and long-range goals.

While the first key result area on the list is profitability, the next six are oriented toward means of accomplishing longer-range goals. Then, in addition, the eighth key area clearly reinforces the importance of balance between long- and short-run goals. Yet, despite this emphasis, neither the president nor any of the men interviewed in this company could shed a great deal of light on how this balance was attained. One found in this corporation the tremendous short-term pressures of profit-center evaluation as a constant threat to the remaining highly subjective, largely intangible, longer-range criteria.

In the profit-center concept of management by results, the decentralized corporation has sought a way of eliminating much of the subjectivity involved in evaluating lower level performance. How does one evaluate the performance of an engineering division or a marketing division? Only by subjective standards and personal judgment can this be done. In the profit center, the divisions are organized so that each controls the major functional elements upon which it depends for profit, and the need for such subjectivity and personal judgment at the corporate level is greatly reduced. The question, "How did the division do?" could now be answered by looking at a most tangible yardstick, profits. Of course, there are disputes on how to measure profit, but such disagreements are quite a bit less difficult to resolve than how to evaluate the performance of an engineering or marketing division.

Having sought in the profit center a way to reduce subjectivity and intangible measures of success, it was not surprising to find that all too often when it came to rewarding managers for success or penalizing them for failure, success or failure tended to be defined in terms of the more tangible and actual results shown by profit, rather than the more subjective key result areas. Recognizing this problem, one survey company created a business measurements group in 1952 as a task force and subsequently made it a permanent organizational component in the corporate accounting service division. Its mission was to develop ways of measuring the more subjective key result areas. A subjective appraisal of its success in accomplishing this mission is that after almost fourteen years of effort, very little has been accomplished. In fact, when several executives of this company were cited by the Justice Department for price fixing, one of the strongest arguments mustered in their defense was that a sense of internal pressure for better sales and profit had left them no alternative than to take this action despite the fact that in addition to being illegal, it clearly was contrary to the company's longer-run interests.

In another of the survey companies, a competitor of the one just mentioned, a similar decentralized management-by-results approach was instituted. Here too, the idea was to give the divisions, and if possible lower levels of management, sufficient resources and flexibility to hold them responsible for integrated, long- and short-run results. By granting them "entrepreneurial" authority, it was hoped they would assume a sense of entrepreneurial responsibility. When interviewing a top executive of the company, however, it was learned that all new product and process research is carried out at the corporate level under a corporate budget. While it is not uncommon for most basic research or research in areas affecting several divisions to be carried out in this way, typically when basic research develops something to the point where *product* or *process potential* is proven, the project is transferred to the division or divisions using this product or process. It is at the division level where final research on feasibility and *market* or *profit* potential is tested. In this survey company, however, corporate management, according to the executives interviewed, had such a tough time getting the divisions to take the risk of carrying new, untested products or techniques that it was decided to take such projects through market test with corporate funds. Then the best bets were turned over to a new products division (also supported by corporate rather than division funds) to get started. The ones that pass the final test, profitable market acceptance, are then offered to the divisions. If they still seem risky, the pot may be sweetened for the division by offering it additional capital as a subsidy or by ignoring the results of the new product for several years when reviewing the division's performance.

As a result of this policy, the "entrepreneurial" division managers are shielded from one of the most important entrepreneurial risks, new product development, in order not to "contaminate" their normal operating results. The approach, while it has certain advantages, also had the effect of reinforcing division management's belief that their major concern must be for the short-run, tangible results and that, for the most part, the long-run is a corporate concern. Thus, division management, which by virtue of their integrated authority was in the best position to see and seek long-run goals, was by corporate action pushed in the opposite direction.

In still another of the survey companies where management by results had created strong divisional profit centers, the following situation was described by a top executive. One of their divisions which specializes in producing large equipment needed a part for one of its newest products. Given the nature of its facilities and personnel, it was not equipped to produce the part itself. Another division, however, had the engineering talent and manufacturing capability to produce the part but was geared up to manufacture such parts only on a mass production basis. To design and produce the part in the small quantity needed by the first division would have been for them an expensive diversion, and so they refused. When the first division insisted that such a part was not available elsewhere and that it was vital to the successful marketing of a new product, the second division reluctantly agreed to produce it but insisted on "adequate compensation." As the head of a profit center, its general manager was not going to "subsidize" another division. When the general manager of the first division saw the "transfer price" he was to be charged for the part, he was almost ready to substitute a much less satisfactory part which was available at a lower price rather than subsidize the other division and have his own short run profit margin eroded.

Fortunately, the problem came to the attention of a group vice-president who was able to act as an "arbitrator." It was feared, however, that such intrusion by the group vice-president merely weakened both division managers' commitment to the profit center concept and so the group vice-president sought to keep such arbitration to a minimum.

The president of this company, learning of this situation, wondered how many others like it had gone by undetected. He recognized that with the management-by-results appraisal system used in his company it was extremely difficult to determine when a manager was taking a short cut to a promotion. He commented during a discussion on this question, "If I could only keep a man on the same job for as long as I hope to hold this one, I know I could get more balance with respect to short and long run."

This sentiment was echoed in several of the survey companies. It was recognized that while some managers would continue to ignore the long range and count on their mountain goat talent for successfully leaping from one problem to the next, most managers would be less likely to mortgage as much of the future to improve their current performance if they knew they would still be managing the same operation when the mortgage came due.

To keep a manager in the same spot for eight to ten years, except at the very top executive positions is, of course, on balance neither desirable nor possible. In the survey companies, division managers seldom stayed on the same job for more than five years. The average tenure was, in fact, less than four years. A division manager in this position is much less likely to worry about his shortsightedness leading to problems three to five years off. He is much more concerned with his short-term performance since he feels these results will determine *his* future. After two years in a post, the manager whose short-term results have been good starts looking forward to promotion. Why should he then take any more risks of investing in the long term than he has to. If they pay off, three to five years hence, under most management-by-result systems, it will be his successor who receives the credit.

On the other hand, if after he is promoted, his successor meets with difficulty, it would be very difficult in most of the survey companies to determine whether this was a result of his poor planning or his successor's poor implementation. Typically, faced with this dilemma, higher management tends to write the problems off as being part of the transition which follows a shift in managers and let it go at that. In fact, it is merely evidence of a second basic deficiency in the management-by-results approach to measuring and evaluating long-range planning activities.

Before turning in Chapter 6 to an approach which attempts to overcome these deficiencies while still maintaining the best elements of the management-by-results approach, consider another aspect of the appraisal programs which are used in the survey companies.

The "Planning Review Approach"

Even in the most highly decentralized corporation, some attention is given to the plans submitted to corporate management as well as to their subsequent results. However, since the emphasis is on "results," only two elements of most five-year plans are given close scrutiny. They are (1) the objectives —primarily, have they been set high enough; and (2) the budget—what will they cost to implement? *How* the objectives will be met, and therefore how, in fact, the budget will be spent, is often given little real attention. To understand why, consider the approach most common in the survey companies for reviewing the elements of the company's five-year plan.

In virtually all of the survey companies the process followed for reviewing long-range *plans* as opposed to results is the same. In only one company has a significant departure from this common approach been tried. This rather unique method will be described in Chapter 6 when looking for a better approach to measuring and evaluating the long-range planning activity. The most typical approach involves essentially five steps. They are listed below, and then each step is analyzed briefly.

1. Preparation of annual and five-year plans at lower levels of company within framework of corporate guidelines.

2. Plans summarized, consolidated, and reviewed at division level.

3. Financial review and consolidation of division plans by corporate budget and analysis group.

4. Substantive review by corporate staff of "prose" plan.

5. Final review with corporate management committee.

Preparation of one- and five-year plans at lower levels

Typically, divisions are required to submit to corporate management both a detailed plan for the coming year and a somewhat less detailed plan for years two through five. In some cases, the plan for years two through five is prepared and presented six months after the one-year or operating plan has been approved, but in most of the survey companies both plans are presented at the same time. In every instance, two basic documents are required. The first is a financial statement (one-year and five-year budget) and the second is typically called the "prose" plan. The formats of the financial plan run the gamut from highly sophisticated and carefully tailored to rather conventional and routine approaches, but basically they represent a translation into financial terms of what the unit expects to do and what resources (both in financial terms) will be required over a five year period.

The format of both annual and five-year prose plans generally called for verbal statements on the following:

1. Key economic and environmental assumptions: Generally these are supplied by corporate management and are repeated and/or modified by sub-units to "show" they were reflected in the plan.

2. Basic objectives of the unit: What the unit expects to accomplish, stated in terms of products, markets, facilities, people and sub-goals for effectively developing each.

3. Operating assumptions: The specific premises and constraints which underlie the unit's plans.

4. Major programs: What the unit expects to do to accomplish its objectives.

In theory, the prose part of the plan is supposed to put muscle and meat around the skeleton of the financial plan. This is usually fairly well done for the one-year plan but is often an almost meaningless combination of platitudes and wishful thinking for years two through five. The reason for this when it occurs is that for years two through five, the units really have no plan but merely a few rather general goals which seem consistent with their annual plan on the one hand and top management's aspirations on the other.

Divisional summary, consolidation, and review

Both parts of sub-unit's plans come to division management for summary, consolidation, and review. Unfortunately, all too often the three activities take place in that sequence, and so by the time they reach the division's general manager and his staff in summary form it may be quite difficult for them to evaluate in meaningful terms the quality of the plans for years two through five. While it is equally difficult for the top divisional group to evaluate the plan for the coming year, time and talent are invariably devoted to this task. As a result, what often goes to corporate management for subsequent summary, consolidation, and review is a one-year plan that has been given a great deal of screening and a two through five year plan that has been given more camouflage paint than anything else.

Corporate financial review

This activity is normally carried out by a section of the controller's department, the budget and analysis group. This section, because of the seasonal nature of its work, is normally too over-worked and/or understaffed to do more than check over the numbers in the plan and in consolidation reflect their impact on the total corporate budget. Occasionally, the group may have helpful suggestions to make in terms of how the divisional objectives may be reached in a more economical way, but normally their efforts are directed toward informing corporate management on the financial implications of the plans. Since the long-range plan often had clear implications on capital management, the financial elements of the program for years two through five get considerable attention. The budget and analysis group, however, is seldom able to do more than study the "numbers" even when they receive the prose portion of the plan.

In theory, it would be desirable to have both the financial and prose portions of the plan reviewed by the same group. In this way, not only would each portion be analyzed on its own merits, but the reviewers would be able to judge whether the verbal assumptions, objectives, and programs described in the prose plan were consistent with the estimations of revenue and cash requirements reflected in the budget.

In one of the survey companies, an attempt was made to have the budget and analysis group undertake both forms of review, and it failed. The feeling was that to find enough men who had sufficiently broad experience to analyze and chal-

lenge assumptions on such things as market research, manufacturing methods, engineering requirements and still be trained
as financial analysts was impossible. If they did succeed in
finding such a man, he was generally whisked away and placed
either as special assistant to a high corporate executive or
placed in merger and acquisition work.

As a result, despite attempts to broaden the backgrounds
of members of budget and analysis groups, they remain essentially number men. They are able to provide management with
insight into the implications of divisional objectives, assumptions, and programs on the company's capital, *only* to the ex-
tent that the objectives, assumptions, and programs given
reflect what the divisions will, in fact, encounter. Since they
cannot provide much assistance in determining how well
thought out the objectives, assumptions, and programs are,
even their contribution in the financial area is really quite
limited.

Substantive review of prose plan

Given the difficulties of having both portions of the plan
evaluated by the same group, the practice in the survey companies is to send the prose portion of the plan to various corporate staff groups for review. The marketing staff would focus
on the marketing issues, manufacturing staff on manufacturing,
and so on. In the survey companies where management by
results was widely accepted by top managements, three related problems arose.

First, since results, as noted earlier, tended to be equated
with profit and short-term, tangible results, the staffs were
motivated to devote most of their effort to evaluating the
first year of the five-year plan. They knew that if they failed
to challenge what turned out to be a weak objective, assumption, or program contained in year one's plan, they would be
more likely, or at least more rapidly, taken to task.

Second, where the staff groups did question objectives,
etc. contained in the second through fifth year of the plan,
they had a much tougher time with corporate management

when challenged by the divisions to defend their position. Knowing that the more nebulous nature of the future would allow them to escape errors they may make in their more distant plans, division managers would argue much more vehemently with staff on such challenges. All too often corporate management in arbitrating such disputes would side with the divisions using the argument that since it would be the divisions who must implement the plan, their judgment should prevail.

The third problem arose in two survey companies when a corporate staff group successfully challenged divisional plans for years two through five. In both cases the executive committee sided with the staff group and required the divisions to go back and revise portions of their plans. Interviews with the staff men who had "won" the debate indicated, however, that they were less than happy about it. One of the men, a corporate director of marketing, summed his feelings up this way:

> It has taken me three years to get that division to make even small strides towards long-range thinking in its marketing operations. The president knew this but demanded a tough review by me. To satisfy him, I had to use a great deal of knowledge acquired by intimate contact with the divisional marketing people. This kind of contact in the past allowed me to be of great help to the division and is also the only way I could dig below the surface of the summarized plan he submitted, . . . but it's all gone now. The division manager rightfully feels that I double-crossed him and from now on, I learn only what I can dig out without his help. I may have helped the president in reviewing *this* plan, but I have given up any chance of really helping that division and because I won this battle I may have lost the opportunity to gain the intimate knowledge of the division needed to accurately evaluate further plans.

As will be seen in Chapter 6 when seeking a better approach to evaluating long-range planning, this problem could have been reduced by not asking the same staff people to do two incompatible jobs, namely aid both the divisions in their planning and the president in his review of divisional plans. In the other case, the situation was almost identical, except that the corporate staff man was the director of planning. Unlike the first case, this man relished the fact that he had shown the president and executive committee what a tough job he had when divisions presented such "poorly conceived plans." Within three months, after he had "clobbered" a second division by "reducing their five-year plan to the heap of meaningless extrapolations and platitudes it was," he was fired. The feeling in the company was that while the director of planning had shown deficiencies in the forward planning of two divisions, the chief executives of these and other divisions were far too powerful to let this zealous, but politically naive, staff expert embarrass them.

Thus, for any of these reasons cited above, the evaluation of the prose plan by staff experts may, using present approaches, fail to provide the insight needed by the top corporate review body. All three of these obstacles will have to be reduced, if not removed, when we turn, in the next chapter, to seeking a better approach to measuring and evaluating long-range planning.

Final review with corporate management committee

As noted above, the nature of this final review has its impact on each of the first four stages of the process. What is submitted from departments and divisions is conditioned by what is expected at the top. Similarly, the nature of both financial and non-financial staff reviews reflects what is expected in the final review. As previously indicated, the final review tends to focus much more heavily on the plan for year one than ensuing years. Review of the plans for years two through five tends to focus on their feasibility in terms of the company's resources rather than the validity of the objectives, assumptions, and propects outlined in the plan. In one of the survey companies, a producer of a variety of heavy industrial products, was the interviewer actually permitted to go over the detailed five-year plans of several divisions and attempt to check, with staff assistance, the soundness of the plan itself.

Following this review and discussions with top management, the following conclusions were accepted.

Arbitrary objectives had been set and budgets designed to "meet" these objectives. When an effort was made to push behind these objectives, it was clear that very little had been done to (1) analyze projections of expected goals so as to set desired goals realistically, (2) analyze the specific problems standing in the way of filling the gap between expected and desired, and (3) design a program of *action steps,* not mechanical allocations of wishful thinking, designed to overcome these problems.

Because of inadequate forecasting, the best possible picture of the expected future state had not been drawn. Therefore, objectives were, to begin with, necessarily arbitrary since they reflected neither accurate projections of the external environment nor in most cases an accurate projection of internal change. Starting without sound forecasts and with arbitrary goals, it is not difficult to see why less was done than should have been done in identifying and analyzing the problems faced in "filling the gap." What is the gap, after all, other than the distance between desired and expected? If the gap cannot be identified, how can problems and needs be clarified, and going one step further, how can programs be meaningfully designed?

What resulted was defended by corporate management as a "first approximation" of long-range plans and a stimulus to longer-range thinking. The five-year plan was seen as a starting point, a point of departure from which the company could make changes as the future became more certain. The chairman of the top management committee stated that while the plans which had been analyzed were quite poor, "Those involved in doing this planning were forced to think further ahead and to reduce to words and numbers a detailed program for the next five years. Although this program may have its limitations and may have to be changed, the people drawing it up were forced to a greater degree of reflection than they would have gone through without this exercise, and their interest in long-range planning has increased."

Contrary to this belief, in discussing long-range planning

with division personnel, there was evidence that perhaps such a view of long-range planning might in fact be having a negative effect at the division level. The feeling was that if top management demanded objectives and programs which reflected the *best* possible guesses about the future, then the fact that they were "first approximations" and subject to change would be quite acceptable. If a best effort is made and falls short of perfection, those making the effort, knowing that their best is expected, will reflect and perhaps be stimulated to make their next effort a better one. Where the best is not demanded and less meaningful efforts are accepted, however, the first people to realize this are those making the effort. When this happens, long-range planning is looked at rather cynically as a time-consuming nuisance which interferes with more important things. A senior staff officer with this company summed up this feeling by stating, "I am not altogether certain that when we work with such imperfect devices and accept such poor plans we may not only be failing to get improved long-range planning, but we may be interfering with those few people whose natural foresight and inclination for future thinking would have been looked to in the past to provide informally what we need in this area."

Conclusions

Thus, the management by results approach, so successful in measuring and controlling short-term performance in even the most highly decentralized corporations, has not succeeded as a practical means of measuring and controlling performance in the longer-range planning area. At present, attempts to add to this approach financial and substantive reviews of long-range plans, while a step in the right direction, have not been particularly successful. Having sought to clarify the reasons for this lack of success, we turn in Chapter 6 to an attempt to design a measurement and control system which overcomes the shortcoming noted in this critique of present approaches.

6

Measurement and Control:

Developing a

Better Approach

In ATTEMPTING to formulate a better approach to measuring and evaluating the quality of long-range planning, one must begin by establishing the criteria by which to judge an effective approach. The approach must tend to minimize, if not remove, the numerous problems encountered in present practices. The following represents a summary of the problems which must be tackled and the means which must be developed to solve them:

1. The approach must reduce or overcome management's tendency to place little real time and talent on long-range plans, because short-term results tend to be the most powerful determinants of managerial success.

2. To do this, the approach must provide top management with the means of measuring the quality and soundness of the *plan* itself or, more indirectly, of measuring the quality and soundness of the planners and the planning process.

3. This must be accomplished in a way which permits management to determine with more accuracy whether undesirable results are the product of poor administration and implementation of sound

plans or whether, *despite* good administration and implementation, results have been poor because of prior planning failures.

4. This evaluation must be accomplished by staff groups equipped to evaluate the soundness of plans, planners, and planning without compromising their relationship with divisions and sub-groups of the company. In addition, the evaluation and recommendations of staff must be made in a way which does not permit lower levels of line management to abdicate from certain responsibilities by citing staff interference.

5. The approach must reflect the fact that while divisional personnel are asked to develop plans for five or more years, they will probably occupy their present position for less than four years.

If an approach which accomplishes these tasks can be developed and implemented, most of the remaining obstacles which are indirect products of present control devices will be reduced, if not removed.

The following proposal reflects an idealized version of what is now being tried on one of the survey companies. In addition, pieces of approaches employed in other companies have been added where appropriate. After an outline of this approach, the approach will be tested by the above criteria, in the final portion of this chapter.

The "Concurrence" Approach at EDC, Inc.

For the purpose of laying out this approach, let us call the survey company which follows it most closely the EDC Company. EDC is a successful producer of industrial products with sales of more than a billion dollars. The company began a formalized long-range planning program more than ten years ago and appointed as corporate director of planning a man with rather unique qualifications. With background in both accounting and engineering, he gained marketing experience in product planning before being promoted to director of corporate planning reporting to the company's chief executive officer. In addition to his technical qualifications, he possesses a rare combination of personal attributes. He adds to an engineering and accounting mentality a philosopher's temperament, a snake-oil salesman's pitch, and a missionary's dedication.

In his first several years as director of planning, he did almost no planning himself but instead, devoted his time to the following activities:

1. Developing a relatively simple yet comprehensive mechanism to be used by the divisions for writing, integrating and revising five-year plans.

2. Selecting the best people he could find to serve as his counterpart within the divisions.

3. Selling to both corporate and lower level management the importance of planning and the feasibility of the approach proposed.

4. Developing an approach to measurement and appraisal which put teeth into the activity.

The planning procedure

Before turning to the measurement and review techniques employed, it is necessary first to look briefly at the planning process employed at EDC. Each year all divisions are required to prepare a two-year operating plan and an equally detailed five-year plan. The two-year plans are submitted to corporate management for review and appraisal in November and, six months later, plans for years three through five, accompanied by ten-year forecasts on key activities. By separating the first two from the last three years of the five-year plan, the company feels it is able to spread the planning load over a longer time period. It is felt that when the entire five-year plan was prepared at one time, the pressures of work made it just that much more difficult to get a fair share of time and effort devoted at lower levels to *developing* plans and at corporate levels for *reviewing* plans for years three through five.

One possible drawback to this approach is that by reviewing plans for years one and two, prior to seeing what is planned for years three through five, it will be more difficult to judge the relevance of the two-year plan to the full five-year picture. In 1966, for example, when reviewing plans for 1967-1968, the company goes back, however, to the five-year plan submitted six months earlier and is able to use it as a fairly good basis for judging the 1967-1968 plan in the context of 1965's plan for years 1969-1970. Thus, even though the focus is on the two-year operating plan, its preparation and review can be related to the five-year plan which was submitted six months earlier. Similarly, when the plan for years three through five are reviewed in May, this review is related to a revised version of the two-year plan submitted in the previous November.

The actual preparation of both the two- and five-year plans follows basically the same procedure as practiced in all of the survey companies. Assumptions on external factors which might influence the divisions are circulated to the divisions along with tentative corporate goals and strategies for the time period being planned. Basic divisional objectives are formulated and tested as to feasibility and programs formulated and costed out. During the planning period, EDC follows, as mentioned, the same basic approach to planning as practiced in the other survey companies. There are two notable exceptions. First, throughout the planning period each division circulates its key assumptions, forecasts, and objectives to the other divisions. In this way, conflicts or possible opportunities for divisional cooperation are made visible before they become more difficult to spot in the summarized statements of detailed plans which will eventually emerge.

Several survey companies have attempted to get this horizontal transfer of divisional assumptions, forecasts, and objectives prior to the development of detailed plans. Unless there is time and incentive at the divisional level to use this interdivisional data, however, this step is wasted and interdivisional coordination must take place later at the corporate level. When this happens, after detailed plans have already been developed and fences built, it is much more difficult for corporate management working with summarized data to do the job effectively. The major reasons for EDC's success in getting interdivisional transfer of data are (1) the nature of the planning cycle leaves sufficient time to use the data and (2) the nature of follow up review by corporate management allows them to find out whether the divisions made use of the interchange and if not, they will want to know why not.

The second difference in the EDC planning approach is that corporate staff groups play a very minor role in assisting the divisions in the *preparation* of plans. As in one other survey company, corporate staff groups will advise and council, will bring in survey material or relevant interdivisional viewpoints but are most careful *not* to give the impression that their major function is to be of help to the divisions. An adequate number of competent people are placed with division staffs, and it is the job of these division level staffs to devote their talents and allegiance to divisional needs. The function of the corporate staff groups is viewed as (1) carrying out corporate level studies, (2) assisting corporate management in formulating and communicating its viewpoints to the divisions, and (3) assisting corporate management in reviewing divisional plans and performance.

By keeping these points in mind, the corporate staff groups minimize the dilemma related earlier. Namely, the case where a director of corporate marketing, after working for years to build the trust needed to help a division, was forced to violate that trust to aid the president in reviewing the division's plans.

The preliminary review procedure

As can be seen from the above, a certain amount of interdivisional coordination and review takes place in EDC while the plans are being formulated. In addition, by giving the division an opportunity to review major aspects of each other's plans, before many important premises and objectives are lost in the summary and consolidation process which follows, the divisions are more apt to uncover for themselves weaknesses and/or opportunities for improvement.

Once the divisional plans have been prepared and summarized (both the two- and five-year plans), they are submitted to the several corporate staff groups. Here, the procedure appears on the surface to be like those criticized in the other survey companies. There are several key differences, however. The financial elements of the plans are reviewed and consolidated by a budget and analysis group as before, but, then, each corporate staff receives not only the portions of the "prose" plan related to its activity but the entire "prose" plan and the financial plan as well. For example, the corporate marketing staff will receive each divisional plan and carefully analyze it in terms of how well it reflects sound long- and short-range thinking in the area of marketing. They must probe beneath the platitudes and seek to determine whether real planning is reflected. Then they must also evaluate the relationship between the prose plan and the financial elements of meeting it.

In theory, this is what might take place in any of the survey companies. Why it often does not lies in these differences:

1. In EDC, the corporate staffs have been built by selecting the very best men in the company in their specialties. The research staff is headed by the most knowledgeable research man in the company. He is not viewed as too valuable to be in staff work. Instead, he is viewed as too valuable not to be. The only exception to this rule would be when the top man in terms of knowledge or expertise lacks the temperament and vision to be more planner and appraiser than doer. In these cases, EDC will settle for the best balance of knowledge and temperament. In many of the survey companies these were not the criteria used in selecting key corporate staff or when the selection was good, failure to provide the following conditions offset proper selection.

2. As noted earlier, EDC makes it perfectly clear that a corporate staff man's first allegiance is to corporate management and only indirectly shall he aid the divisions. While this necessitates capable staff talent at both corporate and division levels, EDC maintains that it cannot afford *not* to pay this price, since the responsibilities of the two levels are potentially incompatible. To ask a man to perform for both leads to built-in conflicts of interest.

3. The corporate staffs are made aware (at times painfully) that they will be evaluated on how well they have forced the divisions to balance their natural propensity to focus on the short rather than the long, on the tangible rather than the intangible. If subsequent review reveals that a division mortgaged its future in, for example, research, the corporate director of research will have a great deal of explaining to do. It is his charge to review division plans in such a way as to minimize the chances of this happening. Since the top corporate staff personnel in EDC are so carefully selected and highly

rewarded they tend, if successful, to have a longer tenure in the same job than divisional counterparts. Thus, they know they are likely to be around when the mortgage comes due.

Given these three factors, corporate staffs carefully probe division plans before they are submitted to final consolidation and review. If one additional step had not been taken in EDC, however, this might be all for naught. The key lies in what happens when a staff head, charged with assuring that long-range excellence in his area is reflected in a division's plan, feels that the division fails to reflect this excellence in its plans. The general managers of most of EDC's divisions are charged with profit center responsibility. If they permit a staff request for change in plan, they *are not* allowed to use it as a reduction or abdication from responsibility. They must not be placed in a position where subsequent unsatisfactory performance can be blamed on the "staff's plan, not my implementation." If this were to happen, then it would be difficult to hold the staff head responsible because he will defend his "plan" and cite "the obvious lack of commitment and subsequent poor implementation of division management" as the reason for poor results.

To avoid this, both parties, corporate staff and divisional management, must come to agreement before the plan is approved and, when this is impossible, state for the record the basis for their disagreement. In so doing, the plan which ultimately comes to final review by the executive committee is one acceptable to both parties; one on which both parties are prepared to stake their futures.

The question which remains is what happens if they can't agree, or more often, prefer not to?

The power of "nonconcurrence"

Since the divisions are charged with profit responsibility and, thus, will take on the responsibility for making corporate staff recommendations work, they should not be forced to accept these recommendations. On the other hand, as has been noted, the staff head, charged with assuring long-run excellence in marketing or research, for example, will be held responsible if subsequent poor results are traced to failures in his area of expertise. Thus, the staff heads cannot be forced to accept a plan which they feel is deficient. Every attempt is made to have two parties who disagree work out a compromise acceptable to both. If this cannot be accomplished, the staff head attaches to the division plan a statement of "nonconcurrence."

In this statement he must indicate his reasons and document them. When this occurs, the head of the division in question will then be required to debate the issue with the corporate staff man before the division head's group vice-president. The group vice president, serving as a mediator, seeks to work out an acceptable solution. Most "nonconcurrences" are settled at this level, but, when the two parties cannot agree, the process moves one step higher. The group vice-president, aided by the division manager, must now debate the nonconcurrence with vice-president of corporate staff, aided by the specific staff head in question. This debate is held before EDC's top management committee, and it serves as final arbitrator. Regardless of how the committee rules, the procedure has forced both the corporate staff head and the division manager to develop fully their positions and document not only their differing programs but the premises and forecasts which underlie them. In the future, when the impact of the decision begins to appear in performance, the availability of the debate records provides top management with a much better basis for judging whether unsatisfactory results stemmed from poor plans or poor implementation or some factor beyond the control of line or staff. This is done by comparing the premises and forecasts (and the methods used for developing them) to what history proved to be fact. It is only fair to note that relatively few disagreements reach the corporate management committee. Both sides in such a disagreement, rather than go through what has to be a harrowing experience, prefer to seek a mutually satisfactory solution. On the big issues though, since both parties know they will be held accountable, disagreements do and should come through this nonconcurrence procedure.

Given these several stages of financial and non-financial

review, the final review of divisional plans by the corporate management committee is a relatively brief one. In theory, by this time, the top advisors to this committee, the corporate staff groups, through discussion and/or debate, have made their views felt. It remains for the committee to check the plans in the broadest terms against their over-all corporate aspirations and resources.

The post-facto review procedure

It would be possible to go through all of the steps described above and still fail to measure accurately long-range planning efforts. The final phase of EDC approach is to review carefully plans submitted in prior years against both present plans and results. Deviations are expected. Only a most conservative or extremely lucky manager will have results which match his plan or will submit in 1967 for, say, 1968-71 a plan which is identical to the plan for that period submitted in 1966. As conditions change, premises and programs must change. Anytime a change is noted, anytime a difference between plans or between results and plans occurs, it must, however, be explained. If a goal for 1969 is set in 1966 and then revised in 1967, the corporate review committee will want to know why. If the manager can show that the premises he made in 1966 were sound, based on information then available, but that subsequent data make them unrealistic then he will have no problem. But, by requiring this explanation, it becomes that much riskier for a manager to throw together, arbitrarily, a plan for three years hence on the assumption that he will do the real planning in two years.

Whether true or not, there are two rumors which persist in EDC. The first has to do with the ex-corporate staff man, whose salary and bonuses had been in excess of $150,000 a year but who was demoted because subsequent reviews of plans he approved showed less than adequate effort on his part to assure long-run expertise in his area. The second rumor maintains that a division general manager who had been promoted to vice-president was demoted to general manager of a smaller division, when subsequent review of plans he had submitted three years earlier clearly revealed that his short-run success had been based on poor long-range planning. The record on two debates he had "won" supposedly showed that while he had been more persuasive, his premises and programs had not been soundly based. Despite his complaint that hindsight is always twenty-twenty, the records and subsequent results indicated to corporate management that the ex-vice-president had had sufficient information when he submitted the plan to have made a better judgment. By not using that judgment, he saved his division three million dollars in costs in his last year as general manager, but as a result, it cost the company an estimated seven million dollars over the next two years and cost him his vice-presidency.

As mentioned earlier, whether these two events actually occurred can not be confirmed. Attempts to check them lead the interviewer nowhere. As he was told, "there's no point embarrassing anyone further." Perhaps they are merely carefully planted rumors, but except for, perhaps, two people, it makes no difference, because most of the current groups of division managers and staff heads are at least willing to believe the rumors about the executives in question are true.

The EDC Approach: Summary

It is only fair to re-emphasize that the EDC approach has been described in its ideal form. Executives in this company still feel much work has to be done to make it work as well as it might. While it will require continued modification and support, it already goes a long way toward meeting the criteria set earlier for an effective system of measuring the soundness of long-range plans in conjunction with operating results. These criteria, cited on pages 79-80, are restated below:

1. The approach must reduce or overcome management's tendency to place little real time and talent on long-range plans, because short-term results tend to be the most powerful determinants of managerial success.

2. To do this, the approach must provide top management with the means of measuring the quality and soundness of the *plan* itself or, more indirectly, of measuring the quality and soundness of the planners and the planning process.

3. This must be accomplished in a way which permits management to determine with more accuracy whether undesirable results are the product of poor administration and implementation of sound plans, or whether, *despite* good administration and implementation, results have been poor because of prior planning failures.

4. This must be accomplished by staff groups equipped to evaluate the soundness of plans, planners, and plan without compromising their relationship with divisions and sub-groups of the company. In addition, the evaluation and recommendations of staff must be made in a way which does not permit lower levels of line management to abdicate from certain responsibilities by citing staff interference.

5. The approach must reflect the fact that, while divisional personnel are asked to develop plans for five or more years, they will probably occupy their present position for less than four years.

The first three criteria are clearly met by the emphasis placed on reviewing *plans* thoroughly before their approval and by the knowledge that subsequent results and changes in plans will be checked against prior plans and deviations will have to be explained. Finally, and perhaps most importantly, EDC is apparently willing to use the output of these planning appraisals as a key element in rewarding and penalizing both line and staff managers.

To meet the fourth criterion, EDC has had to be willing to invest a sizable amount of talent in its corporate staff groups. While they are of little direct help to divisions, these groups, because of their power and potential nonconcurrence, are of enormous, indirect assistance to the divisions by providing incentive to develop sounder long-range plans. In addition, by virtue of the checks-and-balances built into the concurrence procedure, differences between staff and line tend to be integrated, and, where this is not possible, carefully documented reports are available for subsequent review to determine more clearly who was right. This checks-and-balances approach is the key to EDC's ability to reflect the expertise and potentially longer-range perspective of corporate staff in divisional plans without permitting divisions to blame future poor results on staff interference.

The concurrence approach is also the basis for meeting the fifth criterion. The top management of EDC accepts the fact that division managers are likely to remain in the same job for a relatively short time and that their perspective and temperament may, as a result, be more short-run oriented. Therefore, they look to the corporate staff heads, men with longer tenure and longer-term perspectives, to balance any potential divisional short-term opportunism. In addition, the follow-up review of plans and EDC's apparent willingness to trace planning deficiencies back to their authors even when they have moved to new posts contributes greatly to meeting this fifth criterion.

Using the Concurrence Approach in Other Companies

There is no doubt that the attitude of EDC's top management and its ability to man its corporate staff groups with able people are key elements of its approach to appraising long-range planning. The nature of the mechanics of implementing this appraisal program, however, underlies and reinforces these attitudes and EDC's willingness to commit top talent to this appraisal program.

The process may in certain companies requires modifications. EDC, despite its size, has a relatively narrow product line. As a result, it is possible for the several corporate staff groups to apply their expertise to virtually all divisions equally. In a more diversified company, divisional differences in product, market, or technology may make this impossible. In these cases, the role of over-all corporate staff in the detailed appraisal of long-range plans is greatly reduced, and there should be several smaller sets of EDC-type staffs located at the group vice-president's level. Where group vice-president levels do not exist and the staff must be located at the corporate level, then sub-specialists must be found. The basic mechanism and philosophy of checks and balances leading to effective evaluation of plans as well as results and results in terms of plans remains the same.

Any corporation can, with modifications, develop these mechanics and take the first step toward creating the missing link: a soundly conceived and implemented approach to balancing short-term results with long-range plans through meaningful measurement and evaluation of the plan itself. Without such an approach corporate long-range planning is doomed, at best, to isolated and limited success.

Selected

Bibliography

Long-Range Planning: The Overview

American Management Association, "Long-Range Planning in an Expanding Economy," General Management Series No. 179. New York, 1956.
────── "How Possible is Long-Range Planning?" pp. 3-9.
────── "Long-Range Planning at Lockheed," pp. 10-24.
Three good pieces on the issues which underlie long-range planning.

Anderson, Richard C., "Today's Thinking on Tomorrow's Managing," *Business Horizons*, I (Winter, 1958-59), 19-27.
Re-examines several long-standing management principles in the light of changing problems.

Cordiner, Ralph J., *New Frontiers for Professional Managers*. New York: McGraw-Hill Book Company, 1956, 121 pp. (McKinsey Foundation Lectures, "Breakthrough to the Future," pp. 80-117.)
An excellent summary of the need for long-range planning.

Drucker, Peter F., *Managing for Results*. New York: Harper & Row, Publishers, 1964.
An excellent look at the nature and needs of the modern corporation and prerequisites for effective planning and implementation.

92

Ewing, David W., ed., *Long-Range Planning for Management*. New York: Harper & Row, Publishers, 1964.

An updated version of his 1958 collection of articles on planning. Includes fine pieces on long-run strategy and organizing an approach to planning.

Granger, Charles H., "The Best-Laid Plans . . . ," *The Controller*, XXX (August, 1962), 373-76.

A well-written piece on what pitfalls to look for when instituting a formalized long-range planning process.

Hill, William E. and Charles H. Granger, "Long-Range Planning for Company Growth," *Management Review*, XLV (December, 1956), 1081-92.

Pinpoints many of the real values of formalized long-range planning and what is needed to achieve them.

Kitchell, Raymond E., *A Summary of Current Planning Concepts*. Washington, D.C.: U.S. Bureau of the Budget, 1962.

A good job of summarizing the key issues.

Mace, Myles T., "The President and Corporate Planning," *Harvard Business Review*, XLIII (January-February, 1965), 49-62.

Some fine insights into what a president's role in long-range planning is and should be if he can get by on three hours' sleep a night.

Scott, Brian W., *Long-Range Planning in American Industry*. New York: American Management Association, 1965.

A little too pat, but a nice framework and lots of "how-to" hints.

Steiner, George A., "How to Assure Poor Long-Range Planning For Your Company," *California Management Review*, VII, 4 (Summer, 1965), 93-94.

A "tongue-in-cheek" checklist of things to do to assure failure in formalized long-range planning. It's worth more than the chuckles too.

————, *Managerial Long-Range Planning*. New York: McGraw-Hill Book Company, 1963.

Proceedings of a symposium on planning attended by practitioners and academicians. A few real pearls, but it will take a patient reader to find them.

————, "What Do We Know About Using Long-Range Plans?," *California Management Review*, II (Fall, 1959), 92-103.

A first-rate overview of what long-range planning is, what it offers, and what still must be done to make it more useful.

Terry, George R., *Principles of Management.* Homewood, Ill.: Richard D. Irwin, Inc., 1953.
Several fine chapters on goal setting, planning, and organization of the planning process.

Warren, E. Kirby, "Where Long-Range Planning Goes Wrong," *Management Review,* LI (May, 1962), 4-15.
No comment.

Developing Planning Premises: Forecasting
Internal and External Variables

Ansoff, H. Igor, *Corporate Strategy: An Analytic Approach to Business Policy for Growth and Expansion.* New York: McGraw-Hill Book Company, 1965.
An over-all approach to long-range planning, a little heavy on model building, but a lot of clear insight into the process.

Blass, Walter, "Economic Planning, European Style," *Harvard Business Review,* XLI (September-October, 1963), 109-120.
Describes European experience with "indicative national planning."

Bello, Francis, "The 1960's: A Forecast of the Technology," *Fortune,* LIX (January, 1959), 74-78+.
Though not as exciting as Verne or Wells, an interesting look at technological change and its impact on business.

Drucker, Peter F., "The Next Decade in Management," *Dun's Review,* LXXIV (December, 1959), 52-53+.
Not one of his best, but a good article on the nature of what management may expect by 1970.

Ginzberg, Eli and Reilly, *Effecting Change in Large Organizations.* New York: Columbia University Press, 1957.
A real gem! A good short book which gives real insight into the problem described in the title.

Leontief, Wassily W., "Proposal for Better Business Forecasting," *Harvard Business Review,* XLII (November-December, 1964), 166-182.

A little heavy, but not nearly as tough as might be expected from this master of input-output analysis.

National Planning Association, *Long-Range Projections for Economic Growth: The American Economy in 1970: A Staff Report,* Planning Pamphlet No. 107. Washington, D.C.: The Association, October, 1959.

A good set of projections and planning premises but an even better opportunity to see how good such devices are now that seven years have passed.

Newman, William H. and James P. Logan, *Management of Expanding Enterprises.* New York: Columbia University Press, 1955.

Another gem! A good short book on one of the key problems of long-range planning.

Pryor, Millard H., Jr., "Planning in a World Wide Business," *Harvard Business Review,* XLIII (January-February, 1965), 130-39.

A practitioner's look at the entrepreneurial environment and the planning within it.

Quinn, James B., "Long-Range Planning of Industrial Research," *Harvard Business Review,* XXXIX (July-August, 1961), 88-102.

If it can be done, here's an approach.

Warren, E. Kirby, ed., *Management Technology,* The Institute of Management Sciences, v. 4, number 2, Dec. 1964.

Five articles and three panel discussions on aspects of corporate planning.

Wilson, Thomas, "National Planning in A Free Economy," *Challenge,* X (July, 1962), 29-33.

A look at British and French attempts to expand national output through planning without destroying free enterprise. Be careful!

Setting Long-Run Objectives and Strategies

Ansoff, H. Igor, *Corporate Strategy: An Analytic Approach to Business Policy for Growth and Expansion.* New York: McGraw-Hill Book Company, 1965.

An over-all approach to long-range planning, a little heavy on model building, but a lot of clear insight into the process.

Berg, Norman, "Strategic Planning for Conglomerate Companies," *Harvard Business Review,* XLIII (May-June, 1965), 79-92.

A good look at ways of using strategic planning to balance divisional pressures in the light of wide differences in the divisions themselves and/or the men who manage them.

Conrad, Gordon R., "Unexplored Assets for Diversification," *Harvard Business Review,* XLI (September-October, 1963), 67-73.

Goes below the surface in helping to identify a company's or division's real internal inventory of competences. Most useful in planning strategy for growth or diversification.

Granger, Charles H., "The Hierarchy of Objectives," *Harvard Business Review,* XLII (May-June, 1964), 63-74.

Presents an excellent approach to developing a thorough hierarchy of objectives. Permits delegation of managing sub-goals without losing sight of interrelationships.

Guth, William D. and Renato Taigiuri, "Personal Values and Corporate Strategy," *Harvard Business Review,* XLIII (September-October, 1965), 123-32.

As the title implies, a look at how the personal values of key executives influence the strategy of a business.

Kast, Fremont and Sim Rosenzweig, "Minimizing the Planning Gap," *Advanced Management,* XXV (October, 1960), 20-23.

They make a good case for using the framework of a formalized planning program as a basis for developing a faster and more effective decision-making system.

Levitt, Theodore, "Marketing Myopia," *Harvard Business Review,* XXXVIII (July-August, 1960), 45-56.

A classic! Pinpoints need for more long-range thinking. Perhaps it should have ended with a plea for bifocals rather than a telescope.

Long, George I., Jr., "Establishing Company Objectives and Creating an Atmosphere Conducive to Their Achievement," AMA Management Report No. 44. New York: The Association, 1960, pp. 16-23.

The role of participation is viewed along with other devices for developing better goals and gaining greater commitment to them.

Shelley, Tully, Jr. and Andrall W. Pearson, "A Blueprint for Long-range Planning," *Business Horizons,* I (Winter, 1958-59), 77-84.

A good "how-to" article on goal setting and follow-up.

Stanford Research Institute Journal, "The Tribulations of Hawkeye —A Study in Planning," V (Fourth Quarter, 1961), 133-68.

A hypothetical company with very real world problems provides a basis for an interesting and enlightening case study on formalized long-range planning.

Steiner, George A., *Managerial Long-Range Planning.* New York: McGraw-Hill Book Company, 1963.

Proceedings of a symposium on planning attended by practitioners and academicians. A few real pearls, but it will take a patient reader to find them.

Terry, George R., *Principles of Management.* Homewood, Ill.: Richard D. Irwin, Inc., 1953.

Several fine chapters on goal setting, planning, and organization of the planning process.

Tilles, Seymour, "Identifying Goals," *Harvard Business Review,* XLI (July-August, 1963), 112-13.

A good piece on identifying factors which shape a company's goals.

Developing an Approach or Plan for Planning

Anderson, Richard C., "Organization of the Planning Process," *Advanced Management,* XXIII (May, 1958), 5-11.

Several tips on how to organize not only the steps involved in planning but the people who must carry them out.

Besse, Ralph M., "Company Planning Must Be Planned," *Dun's Review,* LXIX (April, 1957), 47-48+.

A fairly good check list on how to plan a planning process.

Branch, Melville C., *The Corporate Planning Process.* New York: American Management Association, 1962.

He tells the reader how to "run the bases" but leaves some questions on how to hit the ball unanswered.

Golde, Roger A., "Practical Planning for Small Business," *Harvard Business Review,* XLII (October-November, 1964), 147-61.

A must on management by crisis. If you aren't big enough to afford a formalized approach to planning and it's too late for genetics, here is the answer.

Hill, William E. and Charles H. Granger, "Long-Range Planning for Company Growth," *Management Review*, XLV (December, 1956), 1081-92.

Pinpoints many of the real values of formalized long-range planning and what is needed to achieve them.

Lebreton, Preston P. and Dale A. Henning, *Planning Theory*. Englewood Cliffs, N.J.: Prentice-Hall, Inc., 1961.

Because of its comprehensiveness, it becomes a little ponderous; but there are a number of excellent insights into the requirements of a sound planning process.

Newman, William H. and Charles E. Summer, Jr., *The Process of Management*. Englewood Cliffs, N.J.: Prentice-Hall, Inc., 1961.

Part III, "Planning: Elements of Decision-Making," and Part IV, "Planning: Decision-Making in an Enterprise," contain discussion of problem-solving techniques worth reading.

Payne, Bruce and James H. Kennedy, "Making Long-Range Planning Work," *Management Review*, XLVII (February, 1958), 4-8+.

The authors set up what they see as the key steps in the planning process and offer a number of good if rather general suggestions.

Schleh, Edward C., *Management By Results*. New York: McGraw-Hill Book Company, 1961.

A good book on balancing the long- and short-run in management. See in particular Chapters I, II and IV.

Seney, Wilson T., "Management Faces the Challenge of Change: How Long-Term Trends Are Affecting Planning and Control Practices," *Management Review*, XLVII (November, 1958), 4-8+.

Includes brief discussion of following planning concepts: the life cycle of a product line; choice among alternatives, maximum-minimum limits; and the dollar model of the business.

Thompson, Stewart, *How Companies Plan*, AMA Research Study No. 54. New York: American Management Association, 1962.

The author presents his findings after three years of studying how companies plan for the future.

U.S. Department of Defense, "Programming System for the Office of the Secretary of Defense," June 25, 1962 (Washington, 1962).

A good look at the "program approach" to planning which has con-

tinued to grow in the defense department and is being pushed into other key governmental departments and agencies.

Organizing and Staffing the Planning Function

Anderson, Richard C., "Organization of the Planning Process," *Advanced Management*, XXIII (May, 1958), 5-11.

Several tips on how to organize not only the steps involved in planning but the people who must carry them out.

Conrad, Gordon R., "Unexplored Assets for Diversification," *Harvard Business Review*, XLI (September-October, 1963), 67-73.

Goes below the surface in helping to identify a company's or division's real internal inventory of competences. Most useful in planning strategy for growth or diversification.

Dufty, Norman F., "The Planning Function in The Business Enterprise," *Journal of the Academy of Management*, IV (April, 1961), 51-58.

A short but useful look at who does what within the corporation with respect to a formal planning program.

Guth, William D. and Renato Taigiuri, "Personal Values and Corporate Strategy," *Harvard Business Review*, XLIII (September-October, 1965), 123-32.

As the title implies, a look at how the personal values of key executives influence the strategy of a business.

Lebreton, Preston and Dale A. Henning, *Planning Theory.* Englewood Cliffs, N.J.: Prentice-Hall, Inc., 1961.

Because of its comprehensiveness, it becomes a little ponderous; but there are a number of excellent insights into the requirements of a sound planning process.

Lucas, Arthur and William G. Livingston, *Long-Range Planning— The Capital Appropriations Program*, AMA Management Report No. 44. New York: American Management Association, 1960, pp. 127-52.

A hypothetical case study of the development of a long-range plan to demonstrate the general method of business planning procedure.

Ross, Ronald J., "For LRP—Rotating Planners and Doers," *Harvard Business Review*, XL (January-February, 1962), 105-15.

An interesting idea but one which takes a rather mechanistic view toward individual and career development. Worth reading even if you disagree with the author.

Stanford Research Institute, *Proceedings* of the Long-Range Planning Service Client Conference held at Menlo Park, Calif., 1962.
See especially pp. 1-23, "Organizing for Corporate Planning," which discusses the findings from an extensive survey of business corporations and suggests a theory of evolution for the planning function.

Steiner, George A., *Managerial Long-Range Planning*. New York: McGraw-Hill Book Company, 1963.
Proceedings of a symposium on planning attended by practitioners and academicians. A few real pearls but it will take a patient reader to find them.

Summer, Charles E., Jr., "The Future Role of the Corporate Planner," *California Management Review*, III (Winter, 1961), 17-31.
A good insight into what is involved in successful planning and what kinds of talents and temperaments need be marshalled to do it.

Terry, George R., *Principles of Management*. Homewood, Ill.: Richard D. Irwin, Inc., 1953.
Several fine chapters on goal setting, planning, and organization of the planning process.

Tomb, John O., "A New Way to Manage—Integrated Planning and Control," *California Management Review*, V (Fall, 1962), 57-62.
An excellent look at the value of explicit line participation in planning and performance review.

Warren, E. Kirby, "The Capability Inventory: Its Role in Long-Range Planning," *Management of Personnel Quarterly*, III, 4 (Winter, 1965), 31-39.

Warren, E. Kirby, "Where Long-Range Planning Goes Wrong," *Management Review*, LI (May, 1962), 4-15.

Financial and Budgetary Considerations

Bell, David E., "How Financial Managers Can Contribute to Better Management," *Federal Accountant*, XII (September, 1962), 9-17.

Hits hard and effectively at the need for financial people to think more of future programs and provide the kind of data and analytical judgment needed to evaluate them.

Capon, Frank S., "Essentials of Corporate Planning," *The Controller*, XXVIII (May, 1960), 218+.
Describes six of the major causes of planning failures.

Jerome, William T., *Executive Control: The Catalyst*. New York: John Wiley & Sons, Inc., 1961.
See pp. 90-114. "Planning—the Creative Force" for a sharp analysis of the relationship of budgeting and planning.

Lucas, Arthur and William G. Livingston, *Long-Range Planning— The Capital Appropriations Program*, AMA Management Report No. 44. New York: American Management Association, 1960, pp. 127-52.
A hypothetical case study of the development of a long-range plan to demonstrate the general method of business planning procedure.

National Association of Accountants, *Long-Range Profit Planning*, NAA Research Report No. 42. New York: The Association, December 1, 1964.
A comprehensive little cookbook worth looking over.

Schleh, Edward C., *Management By Results*. New York: McGraw-Hill Book Company, 1961.
A good book on balancing the long- and short-run in management. See in particular Chapters I, II and IV.

Seckler-Hudson, Catheryn, ed., "Budgeting: An Instrument of Planning and Management." Department of Public Administration, School of Social Sciences and Public Affairs, *American University*, Washington, D.C., 1944-45, v. 6, Unit 4.
A classic on the relationship of planning and budgeting. Don't let the somewhat heavy style prevent you from finishing it.

U. S. Department of Defense, "Programming System for the Office of the Secretary of Defense," June 25, 1962. (Washington, D.C.: 1962).
A good look at the "program approach" to planning which has continued to grow in the defense department and is being pushed into other key governmental departments and agencies.

Index

A

Accountants, and short-range planning, 38
Acquisition planning, 45
Adapting to change, as substitute for planning, 1-2
Ad hoc basis of planning, 16, 24
Affording long-range planning:
  those who cannot afford, 33-34, 35
  those who cannot afford not to, 34-35
Allocation of resources:
  decision making on, 23, 24, 26, 29-31, 36
  and the economy, 13
Alternate programs:
  to government participation in private sector, 14-15
  role of staff specialists in development of, 22, 41
American Management Association, 40
Annual planning for short-range needs, 24
Anshen, Melvin, 13 *n.*
Anticipating areas of future decisions, 30
Anti-trust laws, 12
Appraising long-range planning, *see* Measurement and control practices
Automation, 5

B

Baby boom, post-war, and the labor market, 5
Bach, George L., 13 *n.*
Balance between short- and long-range goals, 66
Bankruptcy prospects, and long-range planning, 34, 35
Berle, Adolf, 12-13, 14
Bibliography:
  developing an approach or plan for planning, 97-99
  developing planning premises: forecasting internal and external variables, 94-95
  financial and budgetary considerations, 100-101
  long-range planning, overview, 92-94
  organizing and staffing planning function, 99-100
  setting long-run objectives and strategies, 95-97
Bonuses, and long-range planning, 59-60
Budgetary considerations, bibliography, 100-101
Budget group review of plans, 73-74, 83
Budgeting, long-range planning confused with, 17, 45, 55-56, 71